A Blueprint for Christian Education

Knowing & Understanding Those You Teach

Donald W. Key
and
Carol Scott

PublishAmerica
Baltimore

First printing

At the specific preference of the author, PublishAmerica allowed this work to remain exactly as the author intended, verbatim, without editorial input.

ISBN: 1-4241-5860-5
PUBLISHED BY PUBLISHAMERICA, LLLP
www.publishamerica.com
Baltimore

Printed in the United States of America

Acknowledgments from Bro. Don

It has been said all that we are is a culmination of all we have experienced and learned in life. This is true when you sit down to write a book, develop a lesson or prepare a sermon. The idea for this book has come after years of preaching, teaching and learning. The need for this book is evident in the Sunday schools and lives of those who attend our churches and educational programs.

There have been many who have contributed to my education both forma and informal. I remember the people of New Zion General Baptist church who were faithful in their service to God when I was a boy. My professors at Oakland City University modeled before me the discipline of study. My grandchildren teach me everyday what unconditional love is; and my wife teaches me patience, tenacity and faith. In addition I wished to acknowledge the hundreds of people whom I have pastured, taught, laughed with, cried with and lived life with. Without these influences upon my life I would not be the person I am today. However, there is one other person who has influenced me more than any other outside of the Lord Jesus Christ. That person is my grandmother Lassie Ernestine Cliburn. She took me and my family into her home, helped raise us children and modeled before us the Christian life. She loved us and cared for us and sought to teach us the value of living for Jesus. I dedicate this book to her memory and to all that she taught me of Christ. Today she is resting in the Lord waiting for that final trumpet call when we all shall be reunited forever.

Finally this book is about Christian education. The kind that we experience at church, at seminars, workshops, retreats, camps, etc. However let us never forget that not all Christian education is in the classroom. God told His people, "And thou shalt teach them diligently unto thy children, and shalt talk of them when thou sittest in thine house, and when thou walkest by the way, and when thou liest down, and when thou risest up." (Deuteronomy 6:7) So we understand that some, and possibly the best, Christian education is outside the classroom and in every day life.

Bro. Don

Acknowledgments from Carol

Although it took about a year in writing this book, the birthing process was about thirteen years. I had always had a passion about teaching and training leaders in all facets of the church, but without this painful birthing process, this book would have never been born.

My husband and I have been in a church plant for the past five years. I teach a class about discovering your spiritual gifts in which I help members identify their gifts and place them in ministry. Following the class, they are instructed to fill out a questionnaire and set up a personal interview. When we meet, we pray together and they share their heart about where God has gifted them. One of the questions I ask is, "What has been your most painful experience?" It's a strange question to ask, but I am reminded that God will never waste a painful experience and will often use these experiences in ministry.

One of the first interviews I had was with a lady who had just lost her 13 year old daughter in an automobile accident. Throughout the interview, she kept asking how God could use such a painful experience into something good for ministry. I prayed and asked God to reveal some things to me and almost immediately, God said, "How can you truly comfort and understand someone's feelings if you have never gone through it?" I shared this with this lady and offered hope that she could be a comfort to other parents who have lost children. Today, this lady is taking classes to become certified as a grief counselor. Not only can she minister within her own church, but she can be available to other parents within the community who have also lost children and are looking for hope.

Who better to send to the jail to do ministry than those who have been there? Who better to teach and lead divorce recovery classes than someone who has walked in the shoes of those attending these classes? Look and see where God is taking you and join Him in His work. Through your painful experiences, God will mold you and make you into a vessel that He can use in His service.

In birthing this book, I look back and see God's hand in all of the struggles He has walked me through. As I was walked through each of them, I questioned God asking why He would allow me to go through such painful experiences. When writing this book, God answered many of these questions.

He said that had I not walked through these painful times, I would never have developed such a desire and passion for teaching and training others. I would have never recognized such a great need and I would never have been able to truly share my heart for ministry. Without the struggles and the trials of the last thirteen years, there would be no book to share with you.

First and foremost, I would like to thank my Lord and Savior Jesus Christ for the gift of salvation and for allowing me to be a part of His work. Despite the struggles, YOU are still Lord of my life regardless of the outcome. Lord, YOU see the big picture and know what's best to accomplish Your will.

I wish to dedicate this book to my husband Mark and my son Andrew, for the countless hours they have sacrificed not having their wife and mom. Mark, I can't think of a greater blessing in my life than to have you as my life's partner. Thank you for being a wonderful husband and father. Thank you for being the great man of God that you are...I love you with all my heart!

Andrew, the most important thing that a mom could ever teach their children is to always seek God first in everything you do. Your relationship with Him is the most important thing in your life. When God chose a son for me, He sent me the very best...you! I thank the Lord for the Godly young man that you've become. I am so very proud of you!

Thank you guys so much for believing in me. Without you, this could not have been done!

I would also like to dedicate this book in memory of my favorite Sunday school teacher, Mrs. Evelyn Gregory. Mrs. Gregory exemplified the true characteristics of the "ideal" teacher and shared her passion to teach about a risen Lord. She not only taught me about God, but planted seeds of desire to reach others. She developed a personal relationship with me and encouraged me when no one else did. Because of her love for God and her willingness to minister the Word to others, she is reaping the rewards in Heaven today. Thank you, Mrs. Gregory, for giving to the Lord. I am so glad you gave!

Carol

Table of Contents

Purpose of the Book

"Go ye therefore and teach all nations, baptizing them in the name of the Father, and of the Son, and of the Holy Ghost." —Matthew 28:19

Christian education in the local church too often has been looked upon as nothing more than an activity. In many instances there is no goal, purpose or structure. Many times teachers have little or no training. They are put into a leadership role simply because there is no one else available for the job. Sunday school is simply something we do before the worship meeting. And yet, we are told in the scriptures to "teach all nations" and to "make disciples." Disciples are learners. They need something to learn and they need to be taught with a goal in mind.

Fortunately, there are many institutions today who are dedicated to making trained purposeful teachers. Unfortunately, much of the curriculum is not geared with the student in mind. Yes, there are lessons plans. Yes, there are desired goals in mind, but how do the lesson connect? What is the overall goal? Are there purposeful objectives that build on each other? Is there an overall purpose that can be seen from the time a child is in the nursery to the time when they become an adult?

For instance, what is an eight year old capable of learning and understanding about the Christian life? How has the previous years of training in the church brought him to this period in his life? And how will the current training contribute to his future training? In other words, how does the entire spectrum of Christian training in the church work together to develop and make this person into a disciple of Christ?

The purpose of this book is to demonstrate the need for and the possibility of a program that is designed with the child in mind and take into account the overall goal of making a disciple. This book will address the questions of the cognitive abilities of children at a certain age and how the teacher can use this knowledge to better educate the student. It will also address teaching methods that lend themselves to more effective teaching and how these methods affect the student's ability to learn.

It is the desire of the authors to better equip our teachers and educators in order that they may learn how to use all of the resources available for more effective teaching; to help them answer the questions that come with teaching. Questions like, "What can we teach this child from the time he is a certain age to the time he reaches another?" It is an aim to help Christian educators and churches develop a program that sets forth goals and objectives for their Christian education program. Our Lord knew his disciples. He knew his congregation. He taught them in ways that made sense to them. He didn't talk above them or beneath them. He utilized a teaching style that took into account who they were, their social situation and their spiritual needs. He is the Master teacher. His methods are reproducible today. His goal was to introduce people to the will of the Father. That should be the goal of Christian education today.

In order to answer the question, "What can we teach this child from the time he is six years old to the time he becomes seven?" We must answer the question, "What is this child capable of learning and understanding?" To do that we must understand the child. This purpose of this book is to help you the teacher do just that.

Part One

The Blueprint

-1-

"A Blueprint for Planning & Goal Setting"

"...that thou make all things according to the pattern shewed to thee in the mount." —Hebrews 8:5

Planning the Structure

Planning for the development of an effective Christian Educational program in the church is much like planning to build a house. The first thing we need to consider would be what type of house we want to build. Will it be Victorian, Early American, Contemporary, or Modern? How many rooms will it have and what will be the function of these rooms? The same is true for the Christian educational program of the church. What it will look like, how many different areas it will cover and what groups will it seek to minister to will be as varied as the churches that undertake to have such a program. In developing your Christian educational program questions such as; What kind of Sunday school do we want, how many classes will we have, where will the classes meet, who are we trying to reach, should be considered. This is the same as asking the question: How much house can we afford and where will we get the money and what type of mortgage will we use.

In thinking of our "house" we need to consider the vision or purpose statement. This statement will keep us on track and help us evaluate our efforts. For instance a vision statement for a house might be: We will build a Victorian style house that will consist of 2400 square feet of living space, with a two-car garage and a bonus room over the garage. This statement defines the efforts of all involved and helps keep them working together for the same purpose. A purpose statement for the Christian educational program in the church might be: We will develop an educational program that will endeavor to reach every age group in the church for the purpose of developing mature, effective Christian who will serve the Lord Jesus Christ. Thus all of our efforts will be evaluated in the light of this purpose statement. Any energy that is not directed toward the realization of our purpose will be eliminated and all efforts that contribute to the reaching of our purpose will constantly be re-evaluated and refined in order to be more productive.

Planning is not everything but it leads to everything. A carefully thought out plan that has been prayed over will result in a more effective Christian educational program in the church.

Considering Our Resources

As you consider building this "house" the resources available to you should be considered. In construction, the type of materials used, contractors available and time of year are considered before construction begins. Likewise, in developing an educational program in the church, many questions need to be answered before the implementation of the program. What personnel is available for your educational needs? Are there enough teachers and assistants available to fill all the necessary classes? What about educational space; are there enough classes rooms that are adequate in size to meet the needs of your educational program? What about a budget? What funds are available for curriculum needs, classroom accessories, teacher training, etc? In addition, time must be considered. When will the classes meet and for how long? All the resources should be considered before implementing your plan. Inadequate resources that have not been considered will result in discouragement among your personnel. Remember, you want to plan for success. To do so you must correctly evaluate every aspect of your plan. Dealing with inadequate resources before you implement the program will be a hedge against discouragement and failure. In addition, your available resources will determine the type of educational program you will be able to implement in your current situation. And a correct evaluation will help you make future plans for improvements or additions to the program.

Gathering Your Resources

After developing the blueprints, determining what resources are available to you, the next step in building a house is gathering your resources. In a house, resources would include materials, contractors, workers, financing, all that is needed to get your construction underway. The same is true in developing a Christian educational program in the church. How will you select the teachers and workers? This will be different in many churches. In some the teachers and workers are chosen by the membership. In other churches the workers are chosen by a board or a committee designated specifically for this purpose. However your staff is chosen they must be gathered together and familiarized with the purposes and plans of the educational program. The "construction team" needs to be familiar with the purpose or vision statement and how what they are doing fits into the overall Christian educational plan. Also, materials such as curriculum, teaching aides, student supplies, etc. should be gathered and made available to the teachers and workers. Contracts are usually a part of the construction of any house. Contractors are given specific responsibilities and a specific time in which to complete their work. Teachers and workers in the Christian educational program of the church should know what their duties and responsibilities are, how they are to do them, when they are to do them, for how long and to whom they are accountable to. They need to be aware of what resources are available to them and how to procure them when they need them.

Everything that can be communicated to them at the beginning will lessen the chance that misunderstandings will occur down the road. So as you gather the resources, especially human resources, communicate, communicate, communicate.

Goal Setting

Once the plans are developed and your team is assembled, the next step is goal-setting. Goals are the means by which we reach our vision or purpose. They are the stepping stones to success. However, setting goals requires wisdom, insight and often common sense. Unrealistic, unspecific and goals that are not time sensitive will result in low morale among the workers and discouragement within the educational personnel. Dr. Elmer Towns in his book "The Sunday School Encyclopedia" teaches that all goals should be SMART goals. They should be Specific, Measurable, Attainable, Reachable, and Time sensitive. Too often leaders set goals that are too vague, unattainable, and unreachable. The result is the teachers, workers and students become discouraged and disillusioned about goal setting. Remember, you want to plan for success. Careful planning that considers the current situation, resources available, and personnel will encourage all involved to reach up and out for Jesus. An example of a goal that is not a SMART goal would be: we are going to have an attendance campaign. This type of goal is too vague. It doesn't answer the question of when, for how long, for what purpose, and what do we hope to achieve. Another goal would be that a congregation of 50 sitting in a rural environment would make a goal of having 200 in attendance the next Sunday. It is specific; it is time-sensitive and measurable. However, it is not very realistic. Is there adequate time to reach the goal? Is there adequate space to accommodate additional families, especially this many? It is too much to expect a congregation of this size in this environment to achieve this goal. When it is not recognized the people will become discouraged and the leaders will not be viewed as wise. A more realistic goal would be this congregation would double in attendance on a certain date in the near future (perhaps three months). This would give ample time to develop a campaign and make preparations for success. When the congregation reached its goal, it would rejoice.

Someone has said, "Aim at nothing, and you'll hit it every time." Without a purpose and without goals to help us reach our purpose then our efforts will not be intentional. And without intentionality in our efforts we have nothing to aim at. Too often we are like the Peanuts cartoon. In the cartoon the characters shoot an arrow at a plank fence. Then they draw a bull's eye around the arrow. Thus they are perfect every time. Setting realistic, measurable goals will enhance our efforts and led to a greater sense of accomplishment among our workers.

Evaluation

During the construction phase of home building, periodic evaluations or inspections are made. This is to ensure that all work is being done according to codes and plans specified in the blueprints. This same attitude should prevail in our educational program. Periodic evaluations should take place to ensure that we are on track, that we are meeting goals and to make adjustments when necessary. Planned meetings where specific questions are asked should be often. Input from workers and teachers should be solicited. Vehicles whereby the opinions of students are delivered should be developed. Attention should be paid to whether or not our people are growing in Christian character, more willing to serve than in the past and whether Bible knowledge is increasing. Are teaching methods being used that are effective? Are teachers and workers on time; do they take an interests in students; are they fully aware of our purposes and visions and have they developed goals that will help reach them? Consistent, conscientious evaluation will ensure that our program is on target and being effective.

Planning to Improve

Once a house is built, the owners usually notice areas where improvements or changes could be made that would improve the home or make it more comfortable. On-going planning should be a part of any educational program. This planning should be for the purpose of making the program better and making the workers more efficient and more content. The question might be asked for what should we plan.

Plan to train. Training is essential. Teachers and workers should be given opportunities to be better equipped to lead their classes. They should be encouraged to take advantage of training sessions in house and off campus. The church should make every effort to include the costs of these training opportunities in its budget and make every teacher and worker aware this is available to them. All Christian education should have as its goal, mature Christian who are willing and able to serve in the body of Christ. This requires training of those who will be leading them in the adventure of Christian discipleship. A good educational program will include on-going training for the teaching staff and those who support them.

In planning for training the following questions need to be answered. Who will we train? This should include all who are in teaching positions in the church, including Wednesday night teachers, men's leaders, etc. Although the teachers may teach different age groups, there are teaching principles that are common to every age group and class. What you want them to know is another area of concern in training. Training should be more than the nuts and bolts of classroom instruction. It should also include development of interpersonal skills, how their particular ministry affects and contributes to the over-all educational ministry of the church. Goals, purpose and mission should be shared clearly and often. Repetition will ensure that everyone is aware of what we are trying to accomplish. Each teacher should be aware of how their class is preparing the students for the next class. Remember our goal is to develop mature Christians who will be willing to serve in their giftedness.

Included in our plans to train should be when the training will take place. Much thought should be given to when and where we will train our teachers and workers. In house training can be done on Sunday morning when the teachers are there. As they are being trained their assistant can lead the class. The next Sunday, the assistant can receive the same type training. Off campus studies may include retreats, seminars, college courses, online courses, and correspondence courses. Wherever and whenever the training takes place should be planned for and then carried out by all involved.

As we carry out our plans, remain faithful to God and His purposes, we will experience growth. Therefore it is important that we plan for growth. Too often we are unprepared for the successes that come our way. Therefore, long range plans and goals that include expansion of present facilities, development of new classes, and the addition of new personnel should be made. Budget requests should be made early enough to allow appropriate consideration of the requests. Deliberate plans should be made to develop new classes that will help grow the Sunday school and youth education in the church. In other words, we should plan to grow on purpose

Conclusion

In this chapter we have addressed the importance of having a plan of action and then carrying out that plan. We have discussed the importance of having realistic, attainable, and measurable goals. We have stressed the value of evaluation and training and how these activities impact the success or failure of our educational program. The rest of this book is dedicated to helping you develop, implement and evaluate your educational program. May God grant us all the wisdom, grace and vision to carry out a plan of education in the church that glorifies His name and matures all Christians to His service.

What Do We Mean by Teaching
or
What is Our Goal or Purpose in Teaching?

It could be said that teaching is the art of imparting knowledge for the purpose of training and preparing. In many instances teaching is used to prepare individuals for a specific service or vocation; i.e. doctors are taught in order that they might be able to practice medicine or perform surgeries. In other words, all teaching has a goal or desired end in mind.

This is no less true for Christian teaching. James Smart in The Teaching Ministry of the Church, declares, "We teach so that through our teaching God may work in the hearts of those whom we teach, to make disciples wholly committed to His gospel, with an understanding of it, and with personal faith that will enable them to bear convincing witness to it in word and action in the midst of an unbelieving world." As one reads this one picks up on at least four objectives or goals of Christian education:

That God may work in the hearts of those whom we teach
To make disciples who understand and are committed to the gospel
To make disciples who have a personal faith and who are committed to
witness of their faith to the world

In other words the goal of Christian teaching is to produce changed lives that in turn will change the lives of others. The Apostle Paul in his letter to Timothy echoed this when he said, "...and the things you have heard from me among many witness, commit these to faithful men who will be able to teach other also" (2 Timothy 2:2). In Deut. 4:1, Moses called the people to listen to the "statutes and judgments" that they might "live and go in and possess the land" which the Lord God was giving them. Jesus' ministry consisted of much teaching. Paul taught in all the churches and instructed his followers to teach other. We are commanded in Matt. 18:19 to teach all nations in order to make disciples.

All Christian educators, be they Sunday school teachers, Bible class teachers, Youth workers, etc. should approach their tasks with the goal of producing changed lives through teaching. This type of attitude will give purpose to our teaching and inspire us to find more effective ways to teach. Without it we are merely spending time. One pastor taped a question on his pulpit in a place where he would see it each time he preached. The question was, "What am I trying to do to these people?" This is the question we should ask as we engage in Christian education. Answering this question will help us to define our goals and purposes in teaching.

Goals Change

It should be kept in mind that our goals in teaching will change as we move from one group of students to another. Early childhood Christian education will be more directed to imparting knowledge of facts and events recorded in the Bible with little emphasis on application of scriptural principles and ideals. As children grow into adolescents, teenagers and then into young adults, the goals of our teaching will change or become more involved with applying biblical truths to our everyday life.

Christian educators should keep these facts in mind as they plan, implement and evaluate their educational programs. Change and more change will be more evident as we pursue an educational program that is geared with the student in mind and not the teacher. The message of the cross should never be dismissed or diluted; however, we can and should implement different methods of getting the message to our students. This involves asking the question, "Is change necessary to better reach the people whom I am trying to teach?"

The Christian education program that is both thoughtful and flexible will be more effective than one that is rigid and uncreative in its approach to teaching people about Christ and God's Holy Word.

Looking at the Blueprint...

The Foundation

Every building has a foundation. Jesus talked about two types of foundations. One he referred to as sand. This foundation was easy to maneuver, easy to level but not very valuable when the storms of life came. As a matter of fact He said that this foundation would not stand when storms come. The other foundation is a rock. This foundation is harder to shape, not easily moved and very valuable in the time of storm. Jesus said this type of foundation would stand in the storm. Jesus said if we would build upon His Word then we would be able to stand in the time of the storm. If we build upon the philosophy of man or the world our house would be destroyed in time. As we think about constructing an educational program in our churches, let us take care to build upon the foundational Word of God.

Building Upon the Word

But how can we do this? What must we do in order to build upon the Word? First we must know it. Secondly, we must believe it. The devil knows the Word of God but he doesn't believe it. Thirdly, we must teach it. Too many times Sunday school is play time. It is just a time for someone to meet with a group and spend time playing games and generally wasting time. While games and other activities have their place in the learning experience, we must remember that we are here to teach the Word and not just to entertain our class members for a while.

Building Upon Relationships

As we seek to build our Sunday school we must remember that relationships are important. Without relationship we have no fellowship. And without fellowship we will not have a very effective ministry. Christian educators, especially those who lead Sunday school classes or Wednesday night bible studies need to realize that their class members need to interact with each other and the teacher in an arena outside of the classroom. If we are to make disciples we must show them we are interested in their lives. We must demonstrate they are more than just a number to us. Sunday school teachers need to be encouraged to have social, evangelical and just plain old fun events outside of the classroom. After all we are seeking to develop disciples who will work together as a team for Jesus Christ.

Building Upon Effective Teaching Methods

No more devastating and detrimental statement could ever be said of Sunday school that, "It is boring." We have the wonderful opportunity to share the greatest news of all time. The Word of God is the most powerful, life-changing book on the planet. However, our teaching of it is many times lackluster, without creativity and without passion. Every teacher needs to learn many different methods of teaching and employ those methods periodically in their class. Some has said that variety is the spice of life. It is no different in the learning environment. Learning does not have to be dull and boring. It can be exciting and anticipated. Every teacher should avail themselves of every opportunity to learn how to teach more effectively and how to make learning an exciting experience.

Building Upon Purposeful Sunday School

Without a purpose we have no reason for being. This is true in any endeavor in life.

Part Two

The Construction Crew

-2-

"A Blueprint For Selecting Leaders"

"Also I heard the voice of the Lord, saying, Whom shall I send, and who will go for us?" —Isaiah 6:8

Selecting Leaders

In many churches the demands and responsibilities of the Sunday school will require the church secure a Christian Education superintendent. This person is responsible for the development and implantation of the entire Christian education program in the church. Often this begins as a volunteer position with the potential for the person to become a paid staff. Attention should be given as to the person's maturity level, spiritual giftedness, personality traits, and their passion. Questions should be asked as to the person's ability to give the required time to carry the responsibilities of the position. Do they like people? Are they a person of the Bible themselves? Are they organized and responsible? How have they carried responsibilities of the past? Were they punctual and thorough in carrying out their responsibilities? Are they a team player able and willing to take direction and give input into the planning meetings?

In addition, the candidate should be informed as to the responsibilities, time commitment and expectations that come with the position. They need to know to whom they are accountable, if there will be any required training they will need to attend, how many meetings per month will be needed to effectively plan for and implement the education program of the church. They need to know the overall goal of the Sunday school and how their position fits into that goal. Furthermore, they will need to be aware of how the goals of the Sunday school come in line with the overall purpose of the church. In addition, they need to know how long the tenure of service will be. Will it be one year? Will they be elected each year? What will they need to do if they feel they are not in the right place? Answering these questions will go a long way to eliminating misunderstandings and misconceptions before they present themselves and will help in preventing problems that might develop in the future.

The same questions, procedures and policies can be implemented each time a new leader is chosen for the Sunday school or the entire Christian Education program.

The Role of the Christian Education Director

The primary function of the C. E. Director is to plan, implement and oversee the total Christian education program of the church. He/ she is responsible for evaluating the church education programs and determining if they are meeting the needs of those who are attending the church. This involves leading the church to have a strong program of Bible study for every age group and other groups within their specific area of service. He/she is to lead the church in developing polices that are used to govern and operate the church education program. He/she is responsible for inspiring and leading the church in Bible study. In addition, the C.E. Director is to assist in making available adequate training for all workers. The director is to work closely with the Sunday school director in planning for the Sunday school and with all the other leaders in all the other educational departments (ie VBS, Children's church, Youth ministry and special or optional classes.

The Christian Education Director is to coordinate the total education program in order that the church might establish goals that involve recruiting new members, conversions, enrollment, and discipleship. The Director should be involved in informing the church of potential workers and involved in encouraging existing workers. Evaluation of curricula and programs are also responsibilities of the C.E. Director. Great care must be taken to insure that all educational materials meet the needs of the various groups that are a part of the congregation. Therefore as the needs of the congregation change the educational program should make adjustments in order to meet those changes.

The C.E. Director works closely with the pastor and all department heads in all the ministries of education. He/she is responsible for developing goals and strategies of Christian education that will lead the church in a strong Christian educational program. Teaching methods, materials and classroom design and efficiency should be evaluated by the Christian education director to insure they are suitable and effective.

This person should be someone who is people-oriented, devoted to the study of the Bible, someone who works well with others, who has a team spirit and who is able to motivate others to give their best. They should be a person who is sensitive, approachable and who is a life long learner.

Christian Education Director

The Christian Education Director is responsible for planning, implementing and overseeing the Christian education program of the church.

Ministry Area / Department	General Staff/administration
Position	Christian Education Director
Accountable to	Pastor
Ministry target	Sunday school / church in general
Position is	Volunteer (with potential of becoming paid staff)
Position may be filled by	Church member
Minimum Maturity Level	Stable, maturing Christian
Spiritual gifts	Administration; Exhortation; Teaching
Talents or abilities desired	Good organizational and planning skills Good communicator
Best Personality Traits	Dependable; Leader
Passion for	Equipping the saints for ministry; Seeing people grow through studying God's Word
Length of Service Commitment	One year minimum

Anticipated Time Commitments

1. Doing ministry / preparing for ministry: four hours each week
2. Participating in meetings / training: one hour minimum a month

Responsibilities / Duties

1. Plan and implement the Christian education program
2. Establish curricula
3. Order curricula and supplies needed for teaching
4. Recruit teachers
5. Plan and conduct meetings, seminars and activities to train teachers
6. Schedule special seminars or classes for specific group needs (divorce care, parenting, finances, marriage enrichment, etc.)

The Role of the Sunday School Director/Superintendent

The role of the Sunday school Superintendent/Director cannot be overemphasized. As John Maxwell has said, "everything rises and falls on leadership". As a leader, the Sunday School Director will have a significant impact upon the success or failure of the Sunday school. His/her leadership will determine the effectiveness of the overall program of the Sunday school. If the leadership is poor and visionless the result will be a Sunday school program that is ineffective and not growing. Therefore the leader of the Sunday school should share in the responsibility for setting goals and casting a vision for the Sunday school. The Sunday School Director should be a person who is knowledgeable, facilitates the work of the teacher, has a vision for the Sunday school and who inspires others to be their best.

Knowledgeable

The Sunday School Director should be a person who is intimately acquainted with the goals and purpose of the Sunday school. Without an idea of the purpose of the Sunday school that is driven by an intense desire for the growth of the souls that attend, the superintendent will be ineffective in facilitating and assisting the growth of the Sunday school. Jesus came to earth with an intense desire to show people how to have a relationship with God that was both real and intimate. This should be the goal and overall purpose of the Sunday school. The director, who has a passion for souls and sees the valuable contribution that Sunday school can make in the Christian life, will be effective in initiating the changes necessary to make his Sunday school program effective and relevant.

Vision

The Sunday School Director should have a vision for the Sunday school and communicate that vision to the teachers, assistants and staff of the Sunday school. He/she should be able to demonstrate to each teacher how their particular role and class can best facilitate and achieve the goals of the Sunday school. This can best be accomplished by having regular meetings in which all the pertinent issues of the Sunday school are discussed. In these meeting policies, procedures, goals and strategies should be discussed. In addition opportunities for training and further development of teaching skills should be shared.

Facilitator

As a leader the Sunday School Director should see his/her role as being a facilitator. He/she should make every effort to make each teacher successful in their particular role. Materials and resources should be adequate and classrooms should be big enough with an atmosphere that is conducive to learning. Periodic discussions with each teacher to determine the material and resource needs for each class should be conducted. The director should then make these known to the person responsible for securing these materials.

Inspiration

In addition, he/she should realize that his/her attitude will go along way in encouraging teachers to do their best for Christ. Often reminders of the purpose and goals and importance of the Sunday school should be given. The director should have a cheerful and humble attitude. He/she should make every effort to acknowledge and encourage each member of the teaching staff. The director should be the leader in developing and implementing attendance campaigns, social events and even Sunday school revivals.

The following example of the role and responsibilities of the Sunday school Director can be adopted by most churches.

Sunday School Director

The Sunday school director will lead and oversee the ministry of the Sunday school. This person will ensure proper staffing, training and operation of the department.

Ministry Area/ Department	Sunday School
Position	Sunday School Director
Accountable to	Pastor
Ministry Target	Church
Position is	Volunteer
Position may be filled by	Church member
Minimum maturity level	Stable, mature Christian
Spiritual Gifts	Administration, Exhortation
Talents or Abilities Desired	Good organizational and leadership skills
Best Personality Traits	Motivated, People oriented
Passion For	Reaching, teaching and nurturing people through Sunday School ministry
Length of service Commitment	One year minimum

Anticipated Time Commitments

1. Doing ministry/preparing for ministry: three hours per week
2. Participating in meetings/training: one hour a month

Responsibilities/ Duties

1. Recruit volunteers to serve in Sunday School ministry
2. Develop and implement a training program for Sunday School leaders, teachers and workers.
3. Obtain information on Sunday school curricula, inform teachers of selection, order curricula.
4. Oversee distribution of Sunday school material or store it in a designated location for easy access by leaders.
5. Recognize, encourage and motivate Sunday School workers
6. Communicate information regarding goals, special days, etc.

7. Oversee operation of Sunday school ministry (teachers on hand, lessons available, start/end on time, records procedures followed/ forms completed, etc.)
8. Serve as a liaison between Sunday School, C.E. Director and pastor

Responsibilities/ Duties

1. Recruit volunteers to serve in Sunday school ministry
2. Develop and implement a training program for Sunday school leaders, teachers, and workers.
3. Obtain information on Sunday school curricula; inform teachers of selection; order curricula.
4. Oversee distribution of Sunday School material or store it in a designated location for easy access by leaders.
5. Recognize, encourage and motivate Sunday School workers
6. Communicate information regarding goals, special days, etc.
7. Oversee operation of Sunday School ministry (teachers on hand, lessons available, start/end on time, records procedures followed/ forms completed, etc.)
8. Serve as a liaison between Sunday school and C. E. Director

In addition the following list of duties of the Sunday School Director will assist in helping define the role.

1. Oversee the planning and the implementation of the Sunday school.
    a. Approve the curriculum used
    b. Enrollment or attendance campaigns
    c. Social events
    d. Sunday school revival
    e. develop goals and overall objectives of the Sunday school

2. Train or provide training opportunities for teachers and assistants
    a. seminars, classes, retreats, etc

3. Make sure each class has a teacher each Sunday
    a. each class should have a teacher and an assistant

4. Make sure the classes start on time
    a. punctuality is a mark of a mature Christian

5. Make sure there are accurate attendance records kept
    a. absentees must be accounted for

6. Be an encourager to all teachers and assistants

7. Make sure that each teacher has adequate supplies and resources

8. Keep pastor and leadership informed as to the successes, problems and needs of the Sunday school.

9. Pray fervently and often for the Sunday school.

-3-

"A Blueprint for Selecting Teachers"

"Go ye therefore, and teach all nations..." —Matthew 28:19

The Role of Sunday School Teacher

The role of the Sunday school teacher is one that wears many hats. They serve not only as a teacher, but as a shepherd, mentor, leader, and friend. Although they incorporate administrative duties such as planning, studying and organizing into their job description, the teacher is the one who puts the Word of God into action before their students. They're the communicators, demonstrators and educators of the church.

The following is a common scenario for a typical Sunday school teacher: He/she is asked if they will consider teaching a Sunday school class. The director tells them how great they would be in the classroom and how the kids would really enjoy having them as a teacher. The individual is asked to pray about being a teacher (some doesn't get time...they are needed today!) When the teacher agrees, they are given the Sunday school curriculum and the rest is downhill from there. They find themselves lost in a classroom with no guidance, no training and no idea what is expected from them.

Sunday school programs are taught by volunteer teachers. Many of them have no formal training, but desire to teach others the Word of God. When selecting teachers, it is important that they understand the 'vision' of the Sunday school program and the goals set forth by the leadership. The teacher must also understand the expectations of the position and the duties required to fulfill that position. A clearly defined job description will give the volunteer teacher clear expectations—before they commit to the task. They'll know what they are committing to and what needs to be done.

A job description should include two things; an overall description of the position available and a list of required responsibilities and expectations. The overall description should be a summary of the position giving a general overview, the title of the position, time commitment and who they should report to. A list of responsibilities and expectations should be given as guidelines that detail what is expected by the leadership of the church for successful teaching.

Job descriptions will vary from church to church depending on the size of the Sunday school, break down of the various age groups, etc...As a general guideline, here is an example of a job description for a Sunday school teacher:

Job Description of a Sunday School Teacher

Job Description:

The overall purpose of the Sunday school teacher is to teach and lead students on Sunday morning in purposeful Bible study. The teacher will also serve as a shepherd and mentor to their students through various events, encouraging fellowship and connection.

Required:

*Be a born again Believer
*Have a heart for teaching and a true desire to see others saved and discipled
*Mirror a life to students that is pleasing to God
*Ability to communicate to students, parents and staff
*Make a one year commitment to teach
*Attend church regularly and support all activities of the church
*Attend scheduled training sessions

Important:

*A team player that understands how all ministries work together to provide for the needs of everyone in the congregation, yet desires reaching children and their families.

*A lifelong learner who embraces skills and knowledge learned through workshops, seminars and training opportunities.
*Organizational skills

Responsibilities:
*Plans and prepares weekly lessons (Estimated average 2-3 hours study, 1 hour planning and 1 hour visitation/follow up)
*Sets goals for successful assimilation of students. Overall goals should include Edifying Christ, Equipping and Evangelizing.
*Plans and organizes "connection" times such as activities, fellowships and special events.
*Recruits and evangelizes to promote their class and the Sunday school

Expectations:
*Arrive to prepare and pray at least 45 minutes before class time
*Evaluate the effectiveness of each class
*Follow up on absentees and needs of students

The Role of the Assistant Sunday School Teacher

There are two main purposes for the Assistant Sunday school teacher. The first purpose is to allow them to be 'mentored'. When an assistant teacher is placed in the classroom, they are able to observe the teaching process and get "on the job training" from the classroom teacher. Also, the assistant is able to assist in the duties of the teacher, allowing him/her to gain experience in the various aspects of teaching. With an assistant, the classroom teacher can focus more on the knowledge being taught and give more individual attention to the student. For personal and safety sake, it is very important to always have more than one adult per class. You never know when an emergency will call you out of a classroom with a student, thus leaving the other students alone.

The second purpose for the Assistant Sunday School teacher is to become the teacher when the classroom teacher is absent. From time to time, the teacher may get sick and have to miss church. The assistant teacher can step into the classroom and teach the class. They are already familiar with the students, the structure of the class and the material being taught.

The primary goal of the Assistant Sunday school teacher is to become a regular classroom teacher. An assistant should not always remain an assistant. They should be encouraged to step out on their own after a period of time and become a classroom teacher. When this happens, they should pull an individual under their wings to mentor, thus making disciples as commanded in Matthew 28.

What are the main responsibilities of the assistant teacher? What are the requirements? Job Descriptions will vary from church to church according to size of the Sunday school. Here is an example of a job description for an assistant Sunday school teacher.

Job Description of an Assistant Sunday School Teacher

Job Description:

The overall purpose of the Assistant Sunday school teacher is to assist the teacher in leading students on Sunday morning. They will assist teaching in various aspects of teaching and assist the teacher in shepherding and mentoring the students through various events.

Required:

*Be a born again Believer

*Have a heart for teaching and a true desire to see others saved and discipled

*Mirror a life to students that is pleasing to God

*Ability to communicate to students, parents and staff

*Make a one year commitment to assist

*Attend church regularly and support all activities of the church

*Attend scheduled training sessions

Important:

*A team player that understands the purpose of Sunday school and works closely with the classroom teacher in accomplishing effectiveness

*A lifelong learner who embraces skills and knowledge through workshops, seminars and training events

*A future teacher in training to become a classroom teacher

Responsibilities:

*Stays in close communications with the classroom teacher in planning weekly lessons

*Assist Classroom teacher with various duties so the teacher can focus on the lesson. Some examples could include preparing an art activity, making phone calls, making copies, etc...

*Prepares and teaches a portion of the lesson each week

*Work with Classroom teacher in setting goals for successful assimilation of students

*Assists in planning and organizing activities, fellowships and special events of the class

*Teach at least one time per month for training purposes

Expectations:

*Arrive early to prepare and pray with the Classroom teacher 45 minutes before class time

*Assist in following up on absentees and needs of students

*Teach in the absence of Classroom teacher

What the Sunday School Teacher Should Expect of the Church

Although churches have requirements and expectations of the teacher, there are some things a teacher should expect from the church. Thomas J. Cook, webmaster of the Sunday school page, gives us some elements every church should offer to their teaching staff.

Support

Prayer support from the congregation, the Sunday school team and the staff. Encouragement and recognition as you fulfill your important task from your Sunday school leadership. Help in solving problems and ministering to your students.

Communication

Information through teacher's meeting, denominational events, and special mailings to keep you informed as a church leader.

Fellowship

Encouragement of workers to participate in an adult class of choice. Fellowship with other Sunday school team members.

Training

Opportunities for improving your Bible teaching skills through a variety of self-study and group settings, through the church and denomination, and opportunities provided through other church-related organizations.

Resources

Provision of adequate curriculum materials, teaching resources, supplies and equipment.

A teacher will only be as successful as they are allowed to be. Knowing they have the support, encouragement and resources will be the keys to their teaching success!

-4-

"A Blueprint for the 'Ideal' Teacher"

"But we all, with open face beholding as in a glass the glory of the Lord, are changed into the same image from glory to glory, even as by the Spirit of the Lord." —II Corinthians 3:18

10 Essential Characteristics of the Ideal Sunday School Teacher

A Sunday school class is only as effective as its teacher. When asked about their Sunday school experiences, many will remember more about the teacher than what was actually taught in the class. That's why it's important that you put the *right* person with the *right* gifts teaching the *right* class. Although it is impossible to have a perfect teacher in place, the following information gives us what is *ideal* in the characteristics of the Sunday school teacher.

1. *The Ideal Teacher Has A Burden For Their Students*

The ideal teacher has a burden for the students they teach. *Webster's Dictionary* defines a '*burden*' as a 'load' or 'oppression'. Not that the students should be a worry to the teacher, but that the teacher should have a genuine 'care and concern' for those in the class. By carrying a burden for their students, the teacher is able to have the following:
a. *Awareness*—The teacher should know the student well enough to be aware that they have a need. This need could be anything from knowing that

something is bothering them and need spiritual advice to being aware of situations and caring enough to want to do something to help. The only way to be as aware as we need to be is to stay involved with those we teach and communicate.

b. *Action*—"They don't care how much you know until they know how much you care" is a phrase that is quite true with those we teach. Actions truly speak louder than words and will be remembered longer. A teacher caring enough about a student to help them through a troubled time will build a bond between them that will carry on through a life time.

A good example is found in Luke 10:33-37 in the parable of the Good Samaritan. The Good Samaritan saw a need, cared for them and took action on the situation. These responses are examples of truly 'taking up your cross' in teaching students the Word.

2. *The Ideal Teacher Commits Themselves to Church Attendance/Activities*

Not only does the teacher teach the Word to the students, but they are a living example of the Word to their students. Students will learn much from the teacher by simply watching how they live their lives. What the teacher does and how he/she handles situations stresses the importance of good Christian habits. For example; if the teacher doesn't come to church on Sunday night or other worship times, this tells the student that worship is not important, therefore 'I don't need to come'. When the teacher faithfully supports and attends activities of the church, they are visually saying "it is very important for me to support our church activities and events." Many students will be at activities and events simply because they will see their teacher and friends there. Many times, younger children are the ones who get their parents to church. They want to be at church so badly, they plead for their parents to take them. Often times, parents are led to the Lord through the efforts of their children.

Luke 12:34 says *"For where your treasure is, there will your heart be also."* This simply means that we prove where our heart is by what we do with our time. Is our time filled with the things of this world, or do we have our priorities in order and put God first in all we do? Where do you spend the majority of your time? Aside from working our daily jobs and taking care of our families, our students must see the importance of setting aside time for

God and giving time to Him with our church attendance, prayer time and study time. Do our students see our priorities in the right places?

3. *The Ideal Teacher's Life Outside the Church Is an Example to Students*

A teacher not only teaches students the Word in the classroom, but they continuously teach the Word by example through their everyday lives. How the teacher handles their finances, refrains from questionable places or publicly speaking of others are just a few of the issues that will reinforce the morals, integrity and character of the teacher. There is an old adage *"Do as I say and not as I do"*. When we speak truths to our students and then they see us living those same truths, students will understand the importance not only because we told them, but because we've shown them. Realizing that we are not perfect, Christian people are often placed under a microscope. The world is watching and waiting for the opportunity to confirm and justify the sin in their own lives simply because of something we haven't handled correctly in ours. Hebrews 4:15 says that Jesus *"was tempted in all things, yet He sinned not."* To sum up the life of a Sunday school teacher, we must *"minister continuously, use words seldom."*

4. *The Ideal Teacher Looks For New Ways To Teach*

The Sunday school teacher will find themselves teaching various lessons in various settings. Even if he/she only taught on Sunday morning, it is very important to teach in different ways. In the Bible, Jesus taught in many different ways. Often He used *parables*, which are short stories used to teach a spiritual truth. There are three parables are found in Luke 15, which I refer to as the 'party' chapter. The stories are; the lost coin, the lost sheep and the lost son. In each of these parables, something is lost, and then it is found. A celebration occurs with those in the story! Many spiritual truths can be pulled from each of these stories, but the most obvious is that of salvation. We are lost and brought back to Christ. A celebration not only occurs with the angels in heaven, but our church body should rejoice that a lost soul has come back in to the fold!

Jesus also taught by quoting Scripture. In Matthew Chapter 4, Jesus was being tempted by the devil in the wilderness. Every time satan tempted him,

Jesus responded with the Word. What can we learn from quoting Scripture? First, the Word is the ultimate weapon against satan. Scripture says that the Word is "...is quick, and powerful, and sharper than a two-edged sword." (Hebrews 4:12) Knowing that the Bible is God's ultimate Truth, we are able to remember God's promises to us as the Word becomes our 'daily bread' and the 'light unto our paths'.

The use of illustrations is another great way to teach Bible truths. Illustrations allow us to take ordinary objects and situations we are familiar with to explain a truth. For example; one way to illustrate the strength one has when belonging to a body of believers is the teacher may take an ordinary 3 foot wooden dowel rod to illustrate a single individual in their Christian walk. Sometimes when trials come against us (the teacher begins to bend the dowel rod...) and we walk alone without the support and prayer of a church family or we don't stay in the Word or pray, the individual may not be very strong (The teacher bends and it breaks in two). The teacher takes a new dowel rod that represents a Christian and adds other dowel rods (calling each one prayer, the Word, a church family, etc...). When trials come against us and we have all of these elements supporting us (teacher tries to bend the rods) it makes it harder for us to *break,* allowing us to stand firm and strong in the Lord! Students will remember illustrations and illustrations will help them remember how it applies to Gods Word!

Use a variety of teaching methods when teaching your class. Don't teach the same way every time! Keep that element of 'surprise' so that students are excited about discovering what you are going to do next! The method you use will largely depend on the setting. If you have a large number of students and you have a great deal of information to share with them, the teacher may lecture. If the class set up allows, the teacher may let students take an active part in the lesson by participating in a 'hands-on' activity. This allows the student to learn by doing. Even doing something small such as teaching from the opposite side of the room can be a change! We must remember that students learn in different ways. Not all students will learn the same way. The teacher must be flexible and not be afraid of teaching their class in different ways!

5. *The Ideal Teacher Spends Time with Their Students Outside the Class*

In a typical Sunday school class, the teacher may have one hour with their students per week! (Some have less than that!) This leaves very little time for the teacher and the students to get to know one another and prohibits relationship building. Teachers will gain many benefits when investing time outside the class with their students.

As the student spends more time with the teacher, he/she begins to build a trust, which will open the door for the teacher to become a part of their lives. When trust is built, the student will feel comfortable talking about things they may not be able to talk to anyone else about. Teachers are *spiritual shepherds* or *mini-pastors* to their class. They are to shepherd and guide their small flock, just as a Senior Pastor would oversee the church flock. The teacher is better able to provide spiritual direction and can ultimately win them to the Lord!

How can the teacher spend time with their students? Much of this time can be spent simply by making a phone call, sending a card or occasionally making a personal visit to their home. The teacher must also schedule activities for the entire class to come together and build fellowships with in the class. Some activities could include skating, Christmas Caroling, doing an outreach community projects or the teacher may plan a picnic or cookout in their back yard! Teachers must spend time with their students outside the class and class connections must be encouraged.

6. *The Ideal Teacher Recognizes the Needs of Their Students*

The teacher must be aware of the needs of the students they teach. Much of this can be obtained through the conversations taking place inside the classroom. For example; the teacher may offer an opportunity for students to make prayer requests before beginning class. When working with children (especially small ones) you'll get prayer requests ranging from "pray for my dog that was hit by a car" to "pray for my dad who just lost his job". First of all, realize that every prayer request is a 'real' concern for that student. When it seems little us personally, it is a big concern for that student, no matter how silly it sounds. As requests are made, the teacher must take note of these needs and do some follow up.

One night I was teaching a group of 3rd graders in a mid-week Bible class. One little girl mentioned that she wanted everyone to pray for her because she was getting braces on Friday of that week. She was very self-conscious about getting them and facing her friends at school. Another student in the class said, "that's a silly request!" I responded by explaining to the students that prayer requests that may seem silly to us, may be very important to those making them. I went on to explain that God not only cares about us spiritually, but in every way…including how we feel about getting braces! We prayed in class for God to give her peace about getting braces and that God would help her to overcome anything she was feeling self-conscious about.

Following class, I met with a couple of students individually and asked them to make a call to her over the weekend, just to let her know we were thinking about her and praying for her. She came to church on Sunday all excited! I approached her to give her a hug and to ask her about her new braces. She gave me a great big smile and said, "The orthodontist told me I could have color in my braces so I had him to use red for our upcoming Valentine's Day party at school!" She smiled showing off the new color in her braces! All of the students thought that was the coolest thing. Many of them were wishing they had braces! I didn't know it at the time, but this was at the beginning of the new 'craze' of color in braces. This girl was definitely 'cool' at school!

A situation happened to me personally when I was in the ninth grade. I played the flute in the school band and someone stole my instrument from my locker. Because my parents were unable to purchase another instrument, I asked my class to help me pray for another way to buy one. After class, my Sunday school teacher gave me $20 to get me started and offered the suggestion that I contact those who played the flute and were no longer in the band. I was able to not only find a used instrument (almost new…they only played in the band a few weeks!), but because of my situation, they were willing to accept $5.00 per week until it was paid for! Not only did my Sunday school teacher give financially to my need, she gave me direction in resolving my situation!

In John Chapter 6, we read the story of Jesus feeding the five thousand. In this story, we find many examples to follow. First, Jesus was on the scene, He recognized their needs and then He met their needs. A Sunday school teacher should be on the 'scene' and be aware of the needs of their students. If possible, the teacher should try and help them meet their need. It may be to make a connection with someone within the church, offer spiritual advice or just be there for them as they trust God for their need.

7. *The Ideal Teacher Sets Goals for the Class*

Before setting goals for your class, the teacher must know something about those they teach. They must be familiar with the characteristics of the age they teach, which allows them to know what they are capable of learning. Also, the teacher must be aware of where they are spiritually so they may be able to build upon it. Everyone in the class will be at different places spiritually. Some will have been in the church all of their lives, while others will just be beginning.

At the beginning of every year, it is important that the teacher find out *where the students have been.* How much church background do the students have? Have they been consistently in Sunday school or have they just begun their spiritual journey? Knowing this information can help the teacher determine where they are spiritually.

The teacher must also know *where they are* in their knowledge about the Bible. This can be done simply by taking a couple of weeks and doing some reviews to see what knowledge they have about the Bible. Many teachers do this in games, puzzles and trivia so that no one is embarrassed because they don't know the answer. The teacher will begin to realize how much knowledge their students have about the Bible and spiritual things.

By knowing where the students have been and knowing where they are, the teacher can begin to set goals on *where they're going*. What does the teacher need to accomplish before the students exit their class? What stories do these students need to know and what applications can be used to help these students discover biblical truths? Other goals can include class attendance, bringing their Bible, challenging students to take what they learning into the community through outreach projects or hand-on lessons. It is not enough to know what the Bible says, but also application must be made, being demonstrated in the lives of those we teach.

Will every student meet every goal and will the teacher see every goal achieved? Teachers must remember that they are planting seeds which may not produce fruit until the appropriate season. Just like fruit trees, they bear fruit according to their maturity and their level of nourishment. The teacher must not become discouraged, but must keep their eyes focused on helping their students achieve their goals.

(See Chapter 11 on Evaluation towards the end of this book)

8. *The Ideal Teacher Spends Much Time in Study, Prayer & Preparation*

A Sunday school teacher is to the student what the Pastor is to the congregation…a messenger of God's Word. The teacher stands between God and the student in presenting the Word of God and will be held accountable for how and what we teach. II Timothy 2:15 says *"Study to shew thyself approved unto God…"* As a Sunday school teacher, we must understand how important it is to be as prepared as possible to teach the Word of God to our students.

Plan a Lesson—Whether you are using a Sunday school Curriculum or teaching directly from the Scriptures, we must PLAN THE LESSON. What is the lesson? What are we to teach them using this lesson? How can the students apply this to their lives? How can I challenge them to use this? What kind of questions will my students ask me about this lesson? The teacher must schedule time throughout the week to study so they may be able to answer questions like these. Find times throughout the week when you can study and get alone with God. Find a quiet, comfortable place where you can lay out your materials. Also, select times when you will be less interrupted by the telephone or the doorbell. If you are an early riser, studying early in the morning may be a more effective time for you. Make your study time a priority and not a 'Saturday night' activity. Remember, students will KNOW if you studied your lesson!

Be Prepared to Teach—As stated earlier in this chapter, many Sunday school teachers spend an hour or less with their students each week. If some of this time is taken to collect our Sunday school offering, take roll and get settled in, a teacher is looking at 45 minutes or less in teaching time! This makes it vitally important for us to prepare as much as possible so that every minute is used for teaching the students. It is important to make a time schedule so that we can accomplish what we've set out to do. We must make a plan then…work the plan!

Arrive Early to Set Up the Classroom—Make sure that tables are clean, chairs are secured and materials are ready. Equipment such as a CD players, overhead projector, etc...should be in place and double-checked to make sure everything is in working order. Pencils should be sharpened and extra Bibles and others materials should be prepared for visitors. Things such as making sure the temperature setting is comfortable and the room is well lighted will make or break your Sunday school class. If the teacher is unprepared, students can and will use this to create chaos and disruption. Being prepared makes the statement "I know what I'm doing. Let's get ready to learn!"

Teacher Readiness

Preparing to teach a class begins the week before. Preparing to teach involves several elements and the teacher should not wait until Saturday night to begin preparing for the class. Most of the time, teachers who wait until the last minute to prepare not only become overwhelmed, but the time and attention has not been given to the students. Therefore, effective teaching does not take place.

Here is a checklist the teacher may use to ensure proper time and attention has been given to the lesson material and the students:

______ Look ahead to the next lesson. This should be done as early in the week as possible so that the teacher can begin gathering thoughts and ideas for the next lesson. Some lessons may give you more ideas, which require more time.

______ Begin praying about the lesson. Pray for God to give you the materials and resources to teach your class effectively. If the lesson is already given, begin praying that God will reveal major points that need to be taught to those that you teach.

_______ Begin praying for your students. Pray for each of your students and their individual needs. As you pray, look at your membership roll and specifically call them by name. Also, pray for those who may visit your class and pray for God to send students to fill the empty chairs in the classroom.

______ Contact your students. The teacher should remain alert and stay on top of prayer requests and events going on with their students. Call these students to pray with them about their need or to check in on specific requests made. If a student is absent from the class, give them a call to check in with them to make sure they are not sick or have needs. When students are encountering tests, events, etc...call them the night before and let them know you are praying for them. Special occasions are another reason to call your students. Birthdays, anniversaries, etc...are great ways to let them know you are thinking of them. Remember...they don't care how much you know until they know how much you care.

_______ Study the lesson. Give yourself plenty of time to study your lesson. If you are using a quarterly, gather more information than is mentioned. Plan ways to make the students part of the lesson. Find ways for students to see themselves in the lesson, making the lesson more relevant to them in their lives. Will you use illustrations? Video Clips? Research? Will you need to gather other materials for students to use in the class? On the average, the teacher will spend 3 hours for every one hour lesson they are preparing for.

______ Last things. Make sure you have everything ready to teach your class before going to bed on Saturday night. Get plenty of sleep and arise early enough to get to church at least 45 minutes before your class is to begin. Remember, expect the unexpected...give yourself time for things that happen last minute!

Classroom Readiness

Time is of the essence when teaching in the church setting. The teacher must prepare the classroom in advance so that they may use their teaching time efficiently. Here is a checklist the teacher may use to insure proper classroom readiness. Don't forget to arrive early to give plenty of time to take care of last minute things and to pray before class begins!

Classroom Set Up:

_______ Tables/chairs arranged
_______ AV equipment ready
_______ Temperature & lighting set

Classroom Materials:

_______ Lesson Materials ready
_______ Pencils/Markers
_______ Teaching resources gathered (Maps, Bibles, etc...)
_______ Copies/Handouts
_______ Teacher Material Ready/Studied
_______ Illustrations/Additional Teaching resources Ready/Displayed

(Once the room is ready, close your door and have some personal time for prayer and classroom reflection).

Pray For the Class—I Thessalonians 5:17 says "*pray without ceasing.*" As you study for your class, pray for God to put the thoughts in your heart and mind that you need to communicate to these students. Pray that they will understand and see themselves in the lesson you've prepared. Ask God to help you as you gather your resources for knowledge on the lesson. Throughout the week, take your class roll and pray specifically for each student in the class. As a teacher, you learn things about them and their lives. You learn about their struggles and their triumphs. From week to week, specifically pray for their individual needs. After arriving early and setting up the classroom, take some time to go around the room and pray for each student that will sit in each of those seats. Some students may sit in the same place every time therefore you can lift their name before God and pray specifically for them. When you come to chairs that are often empty, pray that God will send students to fill them. You may not know their names, but God does. Ultimately, pray for each of your students to come to know the Lord as their personal Savior. Here is a checklist for specific things to pray for in your class;

Classroom Prayer:

______ Pray at each chair for each student. (Most students will sit in the same chair each week). Call each student by name and pray for their individual needs.

______ Pray at any empty chairs. Pray that God will send students to fill the chairs.

______ Pray for yourself. Pray that God will use you to deliver the lesson prepared and that He will give you the words to say and the things to do to accomplish His will for the class.

When everything has been done, stand at your classroom door to welcome and receive your students. Also, this provides opportunity for you to say good morning to those visiting your church as they are being directed down the hall to their class!

9. *The Ideal Teacher Strives to Be a Lifelong Learner*

John 14:26 talks about the Holy Spirit bringing things to our remembrance. When we study and do our part, the Holy Spirit will bring things to our hearts and minds to help us with things to say and do to teach the class. We must be a continual learner.

Surveys have been taken and have concluded that 90% of staleness of the teacher comes from the lack of learning. Most Sunday school teachers are volunteers who love the Lord and love working with children. Most of them are not seminary trained in teaching the Bible nor do they have any kind of classroom training period. Because of this, they are limited in resources and ideas to keep their classroom challenged and fresh. Some who have been teaching for 20 years are still teaching the same way, using the same methods and doing the same classroom activities as they did when they first started teaching. We are living in an ever-changing world with ever-changing people. Teachers must remain current with information about those they teach and strive to continue to learn new ways to reach and teach their students.

There are many ways to be a continual learner. One way is to learn from fellow teachers. As each church has training meetings, teachers can find out what is working for others and implement those methods in their own class. When dealing with a particular issue, asking other teachers will allow one to incorporate their solutions. Another way is to attend local classes and seminars on the Sunday school. Sunday school directors or Education Directors should keep teachers informed of training sessions or classes that may help them in the area of teaching. Also, they may conduct training sessions themselves or have individuals who have expertise in teaching to come and teach the classes. There are many books available that will help in different aspects of Sunday school. Encourage your church to begin a library where books can be purchased help educated teachers within the Sunday school.

One way that has proven most effective to me personally is simply finding out what other churches are doing! There was a lady that I used to teach with who was very involved with the students in her church. Every Monday morning, she would come to school excited about what the students in her church had done over the weekend. I felt like a sponge as I sat next to her 'soaking' up everything about their events and activities. I would ask every kind of question so I could learn about what they did and how they did it. If it was an event or activity that I felt could be done in my class or my church, I would make a plan to use it. Did I do everything they did? No! Did I do everything the same way they did? No! I realize every church has its own people and its own personality. There were things this church did that would NEVER work in mine or vice-versa. I would take the activities and events, and make whatever changes necessary to fit my class or my church. This lady never realized it, but she was truly a resource person for me. Their church did the most difficult part...all I did was use what was already tried and true!

When you stop learning, you start dying! Learn new ideas. Try new things. Don't get in a rut by doing the same things over and over every week. We live in an 'edutainment' society where students are using high tech gadgets to learn. We no longer live in the days of gathering students around a table and saying, "open your book to page 29 and let's read together." Kids want to get involved with the lesson by participating. They want to learn through things and through ways that interest them. They want something fresh, exciting and challenging!

I believe when we do our part to the best of our ability, God will honor that by helping us teach our class. God promises that His Word will not go out in vain, but sets out to accomplish what He intends for it to do. (Isaiah 55:11). His reward for us is a growing class and an eager bunch of students excited about being in Sunday school!

10. ***The Ideal Teacher Guides the Student, Helping Them to Grow Spiritually Through Bible Study/Prayer & Life Situations.***

Growing spiritually is a process that occurs over time. Much of our spiritual growth occurs as we experience things in our lives and as we mature physically. The Sunday school teacher plays an important part in the spiritual growth of his/her students. Students are learning the importance of studying their Bible, seeking God in their prayer life and using what they've learned about the Bible in their everyday life. "Teachable moments" take place when one is able to use a current event or situation to teach a lesson. Teachers do this often in the classroom. Remember the little girl who requested prayer because she had to have braces and a boy in the classroom thought it was 'silly' prayer request? That was a teachable moment for me! I was able to correct this young boys thinking and teach the whole class a lesson on prayer using a real life situation. The teacher will encounter other teachable moments and must take advantage of them to effectively 'seize the day'.

Think about the "Ideal" teacher and the characteristics we've discussed. Evaluate yourself and compare yourself to the Ultimate Teacher, Jesus Christ! If you are called as a teacher, He has and will continue to equip you to do the job He has called you to do. As you evaluate yourself, do you see areas of weakness? Are you having problems being consistent in some of these areas? Maybe you are not spending enough time in study and prayer. Do you need to spend more time in building relationships with your students? You must answer these questions for yourself.

Teachers are developing future leaders. This responsibility is greater than the teacher can realize and so critical that if one generation fails to teach the next, the church would become weak and ineffective. Do not despair, for *"greater is He that is in you us than he that is in the world."* (I John 4:4)

Part Three

The Framework

-5-

"*A Blueprint for Creative Methods*"

"Then opened he their understanding,
that they might understand the scriptures." —Luke 24:25

Teaching with Purpose

Not everyone learns the same. Some learn better by doing than by listening. Some learn best by making application with objects and situations they are familiar with. Some learn simply by listening. Children today are living in an "edutainment" society where they are surrounded by video games, computers and other electronic devices. Sitting children around a table to teach a Sunday school lesson may not be enough to keep them excited about learning and often times proves ineffective.

When teaching, we must evaluate and determine if our students have learned what we have set out to teach them. Let's pretend the lesson is to teach them the "10 Commandments" simply by going through each of the commandments verbally. At the end of the class, I would find a way to determine if they had successfully learned the "10 Commandments". I may ask questions to receive an oral response or I may give a written quiz to determine if they learned what I had set out to teach them. If the class did not learn the lesson, I must re-teach the class at another time in a different way. Unsuccessful responses tell me they did not learn the material presented to them or did not understand the material being taught. My next plan would include teaching the same lesson, but teaching it using a different method. The next time, I may use pictures to teach the "10 Commandments". The teacher should re-teach the lesson until the students have learned the lesson being taught. Once the class has learned the lesson, the teacher should go back from time to time and review their knowledge on the subject. Such reviews can be done either before or after the class.

There are different methods teachers can use to effectively teach their students. Remember, we must not always use the same method each time because not every student learns the same way. We should keep each class fresh and different, even if it's nothing more than teaching from the opposite end of the classroom. This keeps that element of surprise in your students and keeps the class from getting into a rut. A "rut" is nothing more than a grave with the ends kicked out! Many classes are dying because of doing the same thing the same way. 90% of ineffective classes are caused by staleness and lack of resources.

According to scripture, Jesus taught more than He preached. The greatest role model we could have is Jesus Christ Himself, the Master Teacher. We must search the scripture and use Jesus' examples in teaching. As we go through each of these teaching methods, we will understand how each of these can be used effectively and how Jesus used them as He taught.

Lecturing

Jesus taught by "lecturing" many times in the Bible. There were times with only the small group of disciples, but probably one of the most prominent times was when He preached to the multitudes on the Sermon on the Mount. Picture the story in your mind. Jesus was going up the mountainside with His disciples when He saw a large crowd gathering. He probably thought, "This is definitely a teachable moment" and He used it. He had them all to sit down and He taught them. (Matthew 5) I'm sure many sat on the ground while others stood along the edge of the crowd, but I picture the crowd encircling Jesus and leaning in toward Him so as not to miss a single word He said. What was His platform? No doubt He sat on a large rock and taught from His heart.

Lecturing can best be used when there is a large amount of information to be presented by the teacher and discussion is often discouraged. Lecturing can take place with a small group or a large group of people, but there are some factors that must be considered in order to make the lecture method most effective.

The set up of the classroom should encourage listening. In a large setting, the chairs should be set up in a classroom style with rows of chairs, with a podium or table in the front of the class. To help bring the class closer together, seating may be arranged so that the ends of the rows are curved in giving a "let's gather 'round and listen" affect. If possible, include tables so students can spread out their materials and take notes for the class. Walking into a classroom set up in this format visually tells the student that "learning is about to take place."

When lecturing, the teacher must be careful in presenting too much information too quickly. Sometimes we have so much to share that we 'overload' the student making them unable to take notes and comprehend any of the material being presented. When beginning the lecture, give the students an overview of what you are about to accomplish, then proceed by presenting your information. Remember to give them the most important information you want them to know and not fill the class with menial facts. It will be necessary to allow your students time to 'catch up' or get their thoughts back on track at given points. The teacher may do this by stopping and asking a thought provoking question. Students can also be asked to write down their thoughts about a particular point. Jesus used this teaching method often by asking questions. He didn't ask questions because He didn't know the answers, but asked in order to get them to think.

Use visuals, handouts, demonstrations and illustrations to encourage thinking, promote attitude change, help maintain attention and help you to communicate more clearly. This will reinforce the key points that you are teaching them and assist in keeping them on task. Remember, material that is meaningful to the learner is learned more quickly and retained longer.

Lecturing should not always be seen as boring to the student. The teacher must have some excitement about the material being presented and must be organized in their presentation.

Illustrations

Using illustrations is a very effective tool to show relationship between one a physical concept and a spiritual concept. Illustrations are tools that will grasp the attention of your group and help them to remember the points being made in the lesson. In scripture, Jesus used many familiar illustrations to help his audience learn new spiritual truths or to understand old ones in a new perspective. Some include sitting children in His lap to demonstrate His love for little children. He also used them to demonstrate simple faith and warnings about leading His children astray.

Parables were the most common verbal illustrations used in the Bible. In Luke 15 alone, Jesus tells us 3 different stories about 3 things being lost; a coin, a sheep and a son. All three were lost then they were found. A celebration took place because each of the lost things were found. What were the 3 lost things illustrating? Lost souls out of the will of God and being returned and restored. When the lost come into God's kingdom, the church should rejoice because scripture says the angels in heaven rejoice when a soul is saved!

Visual objects and personal experiences can also be used as illustrations. One day, I was asked to sing for a Christian women's group in our city during a luncheon. At these monthly luncheons, they scheduled a speaker, a singer and some sort of activity that appealed to women. On the day I was scheduled to sing, a lady was there with her pottery wheel to demonstrate how she made her beautiful pottery. She had even brought several pieces for the ladies to look at. Normally, while the ladies were eating their lunch, the speaker would speak followed by the guest singer and the activity last. On this particular day, the lady with the potter's wheel had all of their attention, so they asked if she would share about her gift in making pottery first.

From the first word that she spoke, I knew God had something to teach me through her craft. The first thing she did was sit down on a small bench, placed her foot on what seemed to look like the gas pedal of a car, reach down her hand into a large bucket and scooped up a handful of pottery mud and slapped it on a wheel that was going around in circles in front of her. Her first words were, "It doesn't look like much now, but we're going to make something beautiful out of this mess!" My eyes were fixed and my heart was preparing to receive a special lesson from God. I had begun to search my purse for a pen. With no paper, I gathered luncheon napkins to write what God was about to show me.

As the wheel kept turning and with the slightest touch of her hands, a cup began to form from the mud. The lady shared how with certain movements of her hands, she could make the mud into any shape she wanted. With the touch of her hand, the cup became a bowl then the bowl became a pitcher. On purpose, she dipped her hand into the pitcher causing a major flaw. She explained that the mistake was no problem. With a little water, she could smooth out the vessel making it like new again. By this time, I was not only looking for more napkins to write on, but looking for napkins to dry the tears that were running down my face! Up to this point, this is what God was showing me through this pottery making process.

Without God, we're nothing but a mess. It is with His hand that we are created to be something in our lives. Seeing the pottery mud on the wheel allowed me to see my life in the process of being sculpted and molded by the hand of God. The *flaw* in the clay caused me to think about the imperfections in my life and all the mistakes I had made that kept me from being the vessel God wanted me to be. The *water* reminded me how needful it was that I continually cry out for the Holy Spirit to help me each day and how important it was that He guide me so that I can be that vessel God wanted me to be.

As the clump of clay was still spinning on the wheel, it moved off center making it difficult for the potter to work with. She replied, "To achieve a good piece of pottery, it must stay in the *center of the wheel*." My heart began to leap as I thought about how we need to stay in the center of God's will! I sat there at that table praying and asking God to keep me in the center of His will so that I may be able to accomplish His will in me!

The potter completed her pottery piece, and then proceeded to describe the next step of the process. She explained for a piece of pottery to be strong and durable, it must go through a *firing* process. The pottery had to be placed in an "oven" and baked at about 3500 degrees. The Lord revealed to me that it was important for me to endure the "fiery trials" that I must face so that I can grow and be a strong servant for Him. The trials were not to hurt me, but to grow me.

Every woman in the room smiled with joy as the lady concluded her demonstration about making pottery. Their eyes beheld the beautiful, finished pieces, while several inquired about purchasing them. Again, the Lord revealed that my life was bought with a price and that I was truly a priceless piece still in the making! I bowed my head and cried out to God to mold me and make me what He wanted me to be. I prayed that the Holy Spirit would rain down into my life each day, giving me strength to make it though the trials that I must face. I thanked God for the price He paid by sending His Son to die for me so that I may have eternal life.

Although the other ladies were simply enjoying learning about how pottery was made, God was teaching me some great spiritual truths. I was there to sing that day, but before I could sing, I had to share what God had revealed to me in that very room. Not only was I able to tell them how "pottery" related to a Christian life, a visual was there to illustration it as well. Not thinking about my song selection for this luncheon, the music began to play "What A Day That Will Be". What an appropriate song of celebration as we all reflected on the "prize" that awaits us…heaven.

God will speak to us through everyday events if we will just listen. His voice can be heard through the words of our children and He can speak to us through the circumstances of our day. As teachers, we must always be open to recognize and receive God's teaching, whatever form it takes.

Storytelling

Storytelling is a favorite method for teaching children, but is effective and enjoyed by all age groups! Jesus Himself was a master storyteller. His stories captivated multitudes of people, allowing great spiritual truths to "come alive" within their hearts. A well told story will captivate the attention of your students and will allow them to experience what is being told. There is more to storytelling than just 'telling'. You must use descriptive, colorful words and dramatize the story using body gestures and voice fluctuations to give emphasis to important parts of the story. You must be able to tell the story at the student's level of understanding. The storyteller must know how to develop a story, allowing it to build to a climax and conclusion.

When beginning storytelling, the teacher must capture their attention for the introduction of the story. You may begin by making a bold statement or asking a thought provoking question that will get grab their attention. Once the attention is given, the storyteller must do whatever possible to keep their attention throughout the story by being descriptive and allowing the student to visualize the story in their minds.

Begin developing the story by *growing* the characters or telling about the *actions* that are taking place. Let's pretend that we are sharing the story of Abraham and Isaac and you are describing the part of the story where they are getting the mule loaded for the journey to the mountain where Abraham will sacrifice his son. You may describe the setting or may describe what Abraham may have been thinking or feeling as he prepared to sacrifice his son. You may describe how little Isaac was busy getting the gear situated on the mule and running around helping his father whom he loved so much…not knowing that he was the sacrifice. The storyteller must describe the pain in the face of the father, the youthfulness in the activity of the son and even the smell in the air of that bright summer day! When using description, help the listener to visualize color, smells and sounds. The listener may visually see the hidden tears in the eyes of the father and the blue in bright eyes of Isaac as he ran around there busy in the activity of getting ready for the journey. As the story builds to a climax, the storyteller must be careful and not get to the end too quickly. By doing so, many details are left out. The purpose of storytelling is to get the listener to envision the full story in their minds.

To make your story more effective, you must use some body gestures. As the story is being told, the storyteller may slowly walk out into the audience to help capture their attention. They may use their hands to be descriptive. They may use their hands to show about how tall Isaac was or how big the rock was that Abraham sat on as he pondered on what God had instructed him to do.

The storyteller must be able to fluctuate their 'voice', giving special emphasis on what is being told in the story. They must include sounds of excitement, sadness, doubt, anger and other feelings to communicate the emotions of the characters. Also, the way the voice is used will be very important when you take on their role. Isaacs's mother, Sarai, may be illustrated as standing at the door waving her hand as Abraham and Isaac left for their journey. She may have called out, "Abraham, watch after Isaac."

"If you build a campfire, make sure he doesn't get too close. You know how he likes to play in the fire!" The storyteller has to take on the role of the mother and use a 'motherly' voice. Voicing the characters helps illustrate what might have been said and helps the listener to visualize a clearer understanding of the story.

The climax of the story is the *conclusion* or the outcome. The storyteller builds the story, painting a visual in the minds of the student. As the story builds, the listener experiences a turn of events and a resolution occur. For Abraham and Isaac, the storyteller can bring the listener to the point where Isaac is positioned on the altar and Abraham is holding his knife up in the air ready to sacrifice his son. He may use 'role playing' and ad lib conversation that may have taken place between Abraham to God. The storyteller can use his voice to characterize the feelings of Abraham. As the knife begins to come down on the chest of little Isaac, a sound is heard, "baa! baa!" A ram had been caught in the thicket and God has provided a sacrifice so that Isaac could go free!

Don't leave the story at the conclusion. The storyteller should bring their audience to a time of personal decision or discussion. They must allow the story to become relevant to the listener by helping the listener see themselves in the story. Like Abraham, would they be willing to be obedient to God and His will? Are they willing to lay everything aside to put Christ first in their lives? The storyteller may want to leave the story "open" and allow the listeners to go back while you ask "What if this would have taken place?" or what do you suppose would have happened if it happened this way instead? This allows your listeners to think about the outcome of the story and how its circumstances would have changed if it were different.

Storytelling gets better with experience. The more you practice, the better you get at doing it! Stories from the Bible may be told through storytelling, but don't forget neglect to tell stories from your personal life. Your personal testimony of how Jesus Christ saved you from your sins is always an opportunity to share your story with others. Other personal stories may include ways in which God provided for you, brought an answer to a prayer or gave you direction for a particular question. Stories from the Bible are very important to share with others, but your personal story will truly touch the lives of those you teach because you have experienced first hand a problem or situation that those in your class may be going through or have gone through. Listeners want to know what happened to you, what did you do about it and how did God help you through it. Everyone has a story to tell! The Bible is full of the same stories of those who have already gone through situations and tells us what they did and what God did to help them. This allows the Bible to become real in the lives of those we teach!

Teacher-Centered Methods

Teacher-Centered methods include any methods used where the teacher takes the lead in teaching the lesson. Lecturing, illustrations and storytelling are included in the teacher-centered methods because most of the teaching is being done by the teacher. Students will have little or no involvement in a teacher-centered method.

There are 3 misconceptions about learning:
*Listening is learning
*Reciting is learning
*Memorizing is learning

All three of these misconceptions are aspects of learning, but doesn't ensure that learning has taken place. A student may be able to recite the 10 Commandments, but they may not be able to understand what they are and what they mean. Several years ago, my son was studying for a final exam in school. He had several pages of questions for review and I observed him diligently studying for the test. I asked him if I could help him review and he said, "sure". I began to start from the beginning of the review notes and was amazed at the correct answers he gave. He had answered every question correctly! I explained that I wanted to go back through them one more time. This time, I started at the beginning again, then randomly went through and picked out various ones. He began to give me wrong answers. My son had memorized the answers in order and how they appeared in his review notes! I explained that his teacher would mix up all of the questions so that no memorizing of answers could take place. Needless to say, we had to begin our review all over again. Although he had memorized the answers, he did not know them nor did he understand what he had memorized.

From time to time, teachers may find their students uninvolved in the lesson. There will be times when no questions are asked and no comments are given. When no feedback is given, the teacher must continue to discover if the class has learned the material being presented or if they have a correct understanding of it. When students continue to become uninvolved and only hear stories and lectures, they tend to become 'lazy' in the learning process. They *must* participate so that the teacher can determine the effectiveness of the lesson. We must somehow get students involved in learning and help them become a more active participant in the classroom. Here are some examples teachers can get students involved:

Participation: Teachers must take every opportunity to get their students involved in the lesson. This will help better their understanding and allow them to discuss the information in their own words and transfer the knowledge into their every day life. When students begin school, they must be taught to study for themselves. Students in the first and second grade can learn how to locate and memorize books of the Bible and have a general knowledge of specific events that take place in many of the Books. On various occasions, teachers must give their students some assignments in which the student must study on their own. They may be asked to look up a particular Scripture and write its meaning or they may be given questions so that students may be able to look up Scripture for answers. When the teacher encourages the student to study for themselves, they are helping them to get more involved in the lesson being taught and give them practice learning how to do Bible study.

Assignments: Teachers must be careful in making their class too much like "school". Although learning is the primary reason students come to Sunday school, we must not allow our students to feel as though they are going to 'school' six days a week instead of five. When the teacher is excited about the material they are presenting, the students will realize it. The lesson must be exciting enough for the student to want to look for answers and find out for themselves. Much of this will be determined by the attitudes and presentation of the teacher. If the teacher presents it in a way that makes students want to learn and it is something they can identify with, teachers will have no problem getting students involved in an assignment. Some assignments can be given by allowing the students to look up information, surveying individuals within the community and the church, teaming up with an older student to research information, etc...

Student Projects: One of my favorite ways to teach is to plan a project or an assignment, while giving them steps for completion. For example, I took a third grade class and launched a 6 week project called "Project Read". I discovered that my class was not reading Christian material and asked them to choose a book (fiction or nonfiction) that could be read over a 6 week period. The students were asked to bring their book with them and use the first four weeks in reading the book they chose during the class time. Once the book was finished, they were asked to find a teen within the church that would agreed to come to class and assist in completing the last two weeks of the project. Once the book was read, they had to construct a small 'float' depicting the book they had read. On this float, they must display the book and build their mini floats based on what their stories were about. One student had read a book about Solomon's temple and decided to construct a temple made out of sugar cubes. (He even put one of his action figures in the doorway of the temple to represent Solomon!) The students were really excited! With the help and suggestions from the older students, many of them were able to be very creative with their floats. Their floats were displayed on wagons, while another positioned their float on top of a toy car and was driven by the use of a remote control!

At the end of the six weeks, we presented a "Book Parade" to everyone at church. Following a Wednesday night Bible study, we asked the church to come to the fellowship hall for our presentation. With people lined around the walls, each student presented their mini 'float' while I read a short synopsis of what their book was about. (The students wrote these themselves) Each student was given an award which included "most creative", "most interesting", "most dramatic", etc...This project sparked an interest in reading Christian material and impressed upon them that reading can be fun!

Student projects can also include doing research using Bible study aides. The teacher can introduce them to concordances, Bible dictionaries, commentaries, etc...The student is given a topic or a story to research. Once this is done and the material has been researched, the student is able to present their material to the church or even the class next door to them. Since my class was held on Wednesday nights, many times the class was able to assemble everyone in the main auditorium and present their reports. This allowed everyone to gain knowledge not only on one particular subject or story, but introduced a number of subjects and stories to the listeners.

Teacher-Centered methods can involve many ways to teach other than teachers doing all the talking and students only listening. Using a variety of teaching techniques promotes active participation and helps students retain the knowledge learned. When students read it, write it and then apply it, they tend to retain the material longer. Plan lessons that encourage students to read about it, write about it and then participate in an activity that will allow what is being learned to come alive in their personal life.

Student-Centered Methods

Student-Centered methods are methods used where students take the lead in a given lesson or class. Some examples of student-centered methods include using dramas, discussions and field trips.

Dramas are a creative way to teach Bible truths and make the events, stories and characters come alive! Drama is enjoyed by all ages and can be done as a production or in a spontaneous setting within the classroom. Drama can include reading scripts or by simply role playing the part. This method can include costumes and props, but can be done effectively without them. Drama often times allows the teacher to see 'creative talents' come to the surface.

I taught a group of fifth and sixth grade students at our church and we planned and implemented a series of stories from the Bible in which the students used "still poses" with narration to tell each story. Here's what we did...

Our class was quite large, so I choose six stories from the Bible for us to re-create. I divided the class and let the students choose what story they wanted to research. We choose the feeding of the five-thousand, Peter walking on the water, the woman at the well, the rising of Lazarus, the Prodigal Son and the adulteress woman. When the students decided which story or character they wanted to depict, they were given Scripture references to look up and read regarding that story or those characters they were to 'bring to life'. In their own words, they wrote the story as a team. I personally read their stories to correct any wrong thinking and clear up any misconceptions they had. When the story was written, they were assigned a specific area in our fellowship hall where they were to build the scene for the story. They were to find costumes and other items needed to complete their scenes. These students dressed in their costumes and became a part of their scenery by 'still posing' the characters in their story. When the entire class had completed everything, we assigned a narrator to each scene and they read the story that their team had written. The students were challenged to make their story no more than 5-7 minutes long as we would share them all during a Sunday school hour.

When all scenes were in place, we dismissed the classes 5 minutes apart. Each class visited the scene, and then moved to the next scene. Everyone in Sunday school that day, even adults, visited each scene and visually watched each story come alive right before their eyes. No scripts, no memorizing...only watching the characters in the scenes and listening as the narrator told the story. By the time all scenes had been viewed, every person within the Sunday school had been exposed to 6 live lessons from the Bible. Using 'still pose' dramas allowed my students to gain a deeper meaning of Scripture, while allowing them to share what they've learned with others. As a student-centered method, I supervised the project and guided the students as they did the work.

Discussion is another great method of teaching. The teacher must select stimulating subjects from the Bible or thought provoking questions so that students will participate. More participation will take place when the subject or question is something that interests everyone in the classroom.

The teacher must create an atmosphere in which the student feels comfortable in sharing their perspectives and ideas. The teacher must establish some guidelines for the class that must be in affect for every class, whether discussion is taking place or a report is being presented. Guidelines such as; there are no dumb questions...the only dumb questions there are, are those that go unasked. Another guideline should be; there is no laughing or no condescending remarks allowed at any time. Students must not be afraid to share with others, especially in the Sunday school class. A simple suggestion for teachers; don't pretend that you know there is everything to know about the Bible. If you are asked a question that you don't know the answer to, tell the class that you don't know and will find the answer. This will not only allow you to stay on top of things, but it will show your students that you are a continual learner.

Staying on track may be one of the biggest obstacles teachers face when using discussion. We must make sure the discussion stays on the subject being talked about or pertains to what the subject is about. The teacher can wrap up the end of the class by asking them to recall some of the most important facts mentioned during the discussion.

Field Trips are a fun and exciting way to learn outside the classroom. Many field trips can give students great information, while allowing them with hands-on experience! Remember, some students learn better by doing than listening.

My husband and I had moved to Jackson, Tennessee due to his job and we became an active part of a church there. We had Discipleship Training on Sunday afternoons and one Sunday in particular the teacher of the pre-school became ill and could not teach the class. The assistant stepped in and began desperately seeking God and searching for a lesson. It was a beautiful summer afternoon and about ten minutes before the class was to begin, a hot air balloon landed in the field next to the church. The balloon was anchored as we began to run out to meet the man flying this colorful balloon. The man explained that there was a hot air balloon event taking place in a nearby town and he wanted to stop and rest for a while. Not only were we asking God to help us with a lesson, but He blessed us by sending us one and giving the children an opportunity to experience it! With the balloon anchored to the ground, he gave the children the opportunity to go up in the balloon as the teacher shared with them about God's green earth and the beauty of His creation! The children were able to make the lesson come alive and have the opportunity to experience it first hand! This is an example of a field trip that came to us!

Field trips should go hand in hand with the subject matter being taught. If you are teaching on missions, plan a trip to the local Salvation Army or Homeless Shelter and let them see first hand what missions are all about! If the lesson is about loving your neighbor, the class may plan to go and help an elderly person by mowing their yard or raking their leaves. A field trip may include visiting a person who is sick and shut in. Your class may provide cards and letters to cheer them up. Opportunities such as these put action into what we are teaching them. How often should the teacher use field trips? There is no magic number, but try to incorporate at least a couple each year.

There are also some other benefits to field trips which will be discussed in greater detail in later chapters. When students are taken outside the typical classroom setting and more time is given other than the one hour of Sunday school, teachers can begin developing meaningful relationships with students. You can learn more about your students personally and begin building a trust with them. When they have a need in their lives and desire someone to talk with, you may be the one they come to. When they trust you, they will share their heart and you could ultimately be the one to lead them to salvation.

How Your Giftedness Affects Your Role as Teacher

The Scriptures teach us that the Holy Spirit gives spiritual gifts unto the members of the body of Christ (I Cor. 12:11). These gifts are to be used to minister to the body of Christ so that the ministry of Christ is not deficient (I Cor. 12:25). Your giftedness will determine how you teach and how you solve problems in the classroom. For example, if you have the gift of exhortation your teaching will be oriented from your perspective as an exhorter. You feel that all problems can be solved by simple taking the right step first then following its completion on to the next step. If you are gifted in the area of evangelism, your teaching will be oriented toward the winning of souls to Christ. Each one of these views is correct and needed in the church. In addition how you interpret scripture will be highly influenced by your spiritual giftedness. Those who have the gift of mercy tend to be more lenient toward sin than those who are teaching from the perspective of the prophet. It is possible that we may become narrow-focused in our teaching and forget about the value of the other gifts within the body of Christ; so that we tend to see other people's solutions to problems as being incorrect if they do not agree with our own.

Therefore it is important to know and understand the characteristics associated with all the gifts. Understanding your spiritual gift can help you determine where you are best suited to serve in the Body of Christ. Understanding all the gifts can help you appreciate better how others in the body of Christ view problem solving and other needs of ministry within the church.

There have been many exhaustive studies done on this area of the Christian life. These resources can help us determine our spiritual giftedness and teach us how to use them correctly. They can also help us avoid the pitfalls that come with not understanding all the gifts and how they function within the church. One of the most highly recognized is the one developed by Church Growth, Inc. called "Team Ministry". This study utilizes a spiritual gifts inventory along with textbook study. The authors of this book recommend using studies like this or others to help you understand your role in the body of Christ and how your spiritual giftedness affects your teaching style.

-6-

"Understanding the Blueprint"

"Train up a child in the way he should go: and when he is old, he will not depart from it." —Proverbs 22:6

Knowing and Understanding Your Students

The apostle Paul once stated that he became all things to all people in order that he might by all means win some to Christ. What was he saying? He was saying that it was so important to win people to Christ that he was willing to get to know them in order that he might be better equipped to share with them the good news of Jesus Christ. In order to do that he had to spend some time getting to know each group of people to whom he ministered. It was easy for him to identify with the Jews, since he was one. He could identify with the Romans, since he was born a free man in a Roman city. However, the Gentiles were a different story. He did not know them well, since as a Jew he would have sought to separate himself from them, their customs and ideas. However, as a messenger of God he had to learn how to get their attention and lead them to a saving knowledge of Jesus Christ.

It is no less important for us as Christian educators to know our students. How do they learn? What are they capable of learning and understanding? What methods of teaching are the most effective for the students that we are teaching? What methods are not effective? How can we avoid falling into the trap of using the same techniques and methods that we have always used? All of these questions are important and must be answered if we are to fulfill our goal of changing lives for the sake of Christ.

Not only should we know the cognitive development of our students, but we should be aware of their home life and everyday environment. Do they come from a loving home where both parents are involved in their development, or are they living in a single parent home? Is dad involved or is he there but absent? How do the parents at home handle conflict? Is the mom a screamer? Does dad discipline with a belt? Where is each student in the birth order? Are they firstborn, second or the end of a long line of children? Each of these factors will affect how the student learns, behaves and interacts with other children. A child who has been taught that God loves them; that they are born with a purpose and who has been given a healthy self-esteem will be more outgoing than those who come from a dysfunctional household. How the teacher interacts with them is important. Understanding that each person is different with different histories, education and experiences will help the teacher be more effective in their teaching. It will also help the teacher to effectively design the teaching methods and strategies to be used in the classroom.

This will require some time outside the classroom. Each teacher should get to know their students and their home environment. Visits should be scheduled to meet their parents and to see the home situation. Social events should be designed and implemented that will enable the teacher to see how the student interacts with others. In other words, Christian teaching should be a lifestyle and not an obligation only to be met on Sunday morning. The teacher should be interested in the person and not merely caring out a task.

Also, teachers should bathe their teaching in prayer. It is necessary to remember the words of Jesus, "without Me you can do nothing" (John 15:5). Every teacher needs the assistance of the Holy Spirit to empower and enable them in their task. In addition, He, the Holy Spirit, can take the Word of God and engraft on the hearts of the hearers. It is His job to change the heart of our hearers. So it is important that we pray, asking Him to touch the hearts of our students. A teacher can pray for the Lord to change the lives of the students, to help them understand and apply the Word of God to their lives.

Ministering to Infants & Toddlers 0-2

"Explorers"

Children between the ages of 0-2 learn mostly through the use of their senses with touch being the keenest of all senses. He knows different adults by the way he is held. Many studies have shown that children of this age can distinguish their mother's voice from the voice of other females. Sensual gratification comes through their mouth. He may suck vigorously on a thumb or pacifier, eventually exploring the world around him and everything finding its way into the baby's mouth. The infant is attracted by bright, hanging toys and mobiles, encouraging the child to develop his ability to follow objects with his eyes. Extensive studies indicate that early stimulation of a baby's senses actually increases the child's intelligence.

Over the next few months, the child becomes more active and begins to roll and wiggle. He recognizes the faces of his family members and may cry when one of them leaves the room. He is learning to pick up and grasp objects, and enjoys a new skill of "letting it go." One can gain the confidence of children this age by simply taking time to become friendly with them. At this stage, their own distinctive nature and personality are becoming more and more evident.

The "Explorer" is a word that could easily describe this one to two years old child. Giving him freedom to explore the world around them is crucial for learning, but for the caregiver, ensuring the child's safety is of the utmost importance. An atmosphere that encourages learning for the child 0-2 is one that offers lots of space for movement, bright colorful objects to look at and basic toys for play to discover. Playing 'peek-a-boo', reading books with simple pictures, spoons, pull apart and put together toys are among some of their favorites. Closer to the age of two, these children know how to pull off their shoes and socks and are seeking independence. Many are at the beginning stages of potty training and begin building a vocabulary that includes *no.* Their attention spans are very brief, therefore a variety of activities must be offered, allowing repetition due to short memory. Play is very important and learning to share and taking turns should be encouraged because they only see themselves in their little 'world'.

The needs of an infant can be easily summarized. His physical needs must be met, and they must be met in an atmosphere of love and by those who love him. "Spiritual, mental, emotional, and social development hinge upon the way physical needs are met." As the physical needs of the child are met, a sense of security is established, building trust with those who care for them. Long before he knows anything about what is *taught,* he will know how he *feels*.

As the worker gently holds the infant and is speaking in a loving, compassionate way, the child learns that he is safe and loved. The nursery worker has an awesome responsibility of helping the child to establish the first impressions of the *church.*

The nursery (0-2) provides excellent opportunities for ministry not only to the child, but also to the child's family. This single ministry can open more ministry doors than any other ministry within the church. The objective of this ministry "is not to *relieve* parents from their responsibilities for the religious training of their children, but to *help them* fulfill those responsibilities. First, nursery ministries reach children, but it provides an open 'invitation' to make a home visit and welcome them into the church. Second, the nursery provides care for the children during regular teaching and worship times, allowing the church to provide solid biblical teaching and training. Third, the nursery ministry allows parents and family to participate in the services provided by the church. According to Meryl Welch, "growths of 35 percent to 65 percent have been attributed to this one department" making this an open door of opportunity!

Connecting to the Bible

Now that we understand the development of children ages 0-2, let's make a connection in how they can effectively learn about spiritual things.

Previously, we learned that children of this age can be best ministered to by simply meeting their physical needs and providing an atmosphere of love. They learn through their senses and 'explore' through movement. Biblical foundations of these children are best learned through their environment and the actions of their caregivers. The nursery is their first impression of *"church"* and we must teach Christ to them simply through words and action.

The *key* word to remember when working with these children is *foundation.* The church must provide ways in which to teach a basic foundation of Jesus and the church through simple words and actions. When parents bring their children to their nursery class, it is important that the child be met by a gentle, caring worker who understands the needs of children of this age. Not only does it provide a sense of safety and trust for the child, but it leaves the parents encouraged and worry-free that their children will be taken care of and ministered to. Upon receiving these children, the workers must verbalize their excitement of what is about to take place in the classroom. "Good morning little Johnny, we are so glad that you came to learn about Jesus today!" In time, the child learns that when they come to church, they are received in love and will be excited in learning about Jesus.

The worker can incorporate other opportunities for the child to learn about Jesus and the church through simple gestures. Before the child is to be fed, the worker can tell the infant that Jesus loves us so much that He provided good food to keep us healthy. The worker should offer a short prayer giving thanks for the food. A prayer could be one such as this; "Thank you Jesus for our food and keeping us healthy, Amen." As this is repeated, the child will begin to learn that we should thank Jesus for our food. What a great foundation we are establishing with our children regarding prayer! The worker can talk to the infant about how Jesus loves them and how He blesses us through other activities such as diaper changing and playtime by simply making a connection with what is being done and how Jesus provides that for us.

Another opportunity is one that is more obvious...the rocking chair! The rocking chair is not only used to soothe a crying baby, but should also be used to communicate God's Word. As the child is being rocked, the worker can sing simple songs that will teach about Jesus and His Word. "Jesus Loves Me" or "This Is the Day That the Lord Has Made" and "Jesus Loves the Little Children of the World" are excellent songs to sing! Through these actions, the child is *feeling* loved through the actions of the worker and being *taught* some basic foundational principals through something they love...*singing!*

The ministry of children should be more than babysitting to the church. Parents must realize that this is where the foundation is laid and the remaining church *experiences* will rest upon it. The child will begin to learn what the rest of the church is like. We have an excellent opportunity to teach foundational principals that will carry on with them through their lifetime.

The Church Supports the Home

The church is not to replace the home by any means, but should be a support to what is being taught in the home. The church can help the parent teach the child more about Jesus by simply having the parent do what the church is doing in the home! Discuss with the parents the purpose of what is being taught in the nursery class and encourage the parents to mirror those things in the home. Encourage them to begin saying a blessing over the food before each meal, set aside a little 'devotion' time by means of the rocking chair and making a connection between what is being said and done with God's Word. The church and the home must work together in providing a solid biblical foundation for children.

The church can be a support of the home by providing helpful resources to the parents by means of the church or activities within the community. The church may host a parenting class or other classes related to the care and education of children and make them available to parents within the church and in the community. Other local organizations may offer babysitting classes, CPR classes or basic first-aid and safety courses in which the church can help sponsor and provide. Local health organizations such as the area hospital or children's medical professionals may provide some helpful brochures or booklets that you can pass along to the parents of these little ones free of charge. When the church provides and supports needed programs such as these, it sends a message to our families that they care about the child not only spiritually, but physically and emotionally as well.

As children are enrolled in the nursery program, a visit can be made to the home of the child. The worker may take an appreciation gift such as a certificate or a small New Testament as a gift from the church. A Polaroid picture of the child's first day in the nursery is another great idea. Parents will not only accept these gifts of appreciation, but will keep them as keepsakes of the child. Parents will gain a greater appreciation not only for the workers of this ministry, but the church as well because they love and care about their children! This visit is a great time to share about other ministries within the church that other family members may not be aware of.

Notes to the Teacher

Don't make the ministry of these children merely babysitting! The following is a typical scenario in a church ministering to this age group; the church has 2 or three workers in this area who show up late to teach class. No preparation is made in getting ready for these children. As they receive the children, the worker is more involved in conversation with other adults regarding things that don't involve information about the child. As long as these children are not crying or demanding attention, they are placed in bouncy seats and cribs to accommodate them and the workers end up sitting in the rocking chairs in conversation about things they encountered over the past week! Don't allow your nursery ministry to become like this!

Have your workers to arrive at least 30 minutes early to prepare the classroom and to pray for the ministry that is about to take place. It's a great idea to have music playing and the room set up for learning! As each child arrives, let the focus of the worker be on each individual child. As each child arrives, there should be a one on one relationship between them and the teacher. This teaches the child that they are very important to the worker and parents will appreciate this. The workers may have an idea of how many children to expect and should rotate in receiving them, giving them ample time to get them settled in before receiving another one. Once the worker has received his/her children, their focus must be on those students, taking every opportunity to teach them for the duration of the class.

As the children are picked up after class, inform the parents about things you did with them during their time with you. Encourage the parents to do those same things with their child throughout the week to support what was taught to them at church.

Helpful Ideas for Ministering to Children 0-2

Room Preparation

Preparing the room for learning before children arrive will give the worker a more time effective and productive class. Here are some of the items a worker may want to check before children begin arriving;

*Changing table is clean and ready for use. Make sure there are plenty of wipes and other necessary items available for diaper changing.
*Bouncy seats and high chairs are clean and ready for use.
*Rocking chairs are positioned so that little fingers and toes will not be in the way.

*Baby beds have clean sheets and blankets.
*Snacks are ready and available for the older infant as needed
*Appropriate books and toys are clean and ready for use
*Soft music may be playing upon the arrival of the younger child or a lively music CD or DVD may be playing for the older infant.

Ministering from the Rocking Chair

A worker may minister to an infant in a variety of way from the rocking chair! Whether it be through feeding the child a bottle or simply by holding them close to comfort them to help them fall asleep, the rocking chair can probably be one of the best ministry tools in the nursery! Here are some helpful guidelines to use when ministering from the rocking chair:

*Before giving a bottle, offer a short prayer of thanksgiving for the food. This is a great way to begin teaching the child to say the blessing before the food.
*When rocking the infant to soothe them, hold them close and begin to sing soft lullaby's such as "Jesus Loves Me". Other songs sang in the church can also be used. Some favorites include: "Where Could I Go But to the Lord", "Amazing Grace" and "Tis So Sweet To Trust In Jesus". If the worker shies away from singing, they may choose to hum or play a baby lullaby CD.

Ministering from the Changing Table

Ministry to infants can simply take place through connecting our actions with the child, with Jesus and the Bible.

*When the worker is changing the child's diaper, they may talk to the infant about how we want to help them stay safe and dry. The worker can then express how Jesus wants to take care of us by keeping us safe in His care by watching over us.
*The worker may count the child's little fingers and toes out loud and teaching explaining that not only do we have 10 fingers and toes, but Jesus gives us 10 commandments to live by.

*Express to the child how they are growing everyday. Connect this by expressing to the child that Jesus came to the earth just like them...as a little baby. Jesus wants us to grow up big and strong and wants them to grow up and serve Him.

Note: A great sign to place above the changing table:

"We shall not all sleep, but we shall all be changed." I Cor. 15:51

Ministering Within the Classroom

Ministry within this age group is more *felt* than *taught.* The worker must remember to make connections with what they are doing with Jesus and His Word. Books, toys, mobiles, etc...gives the worker an opportunity to take an ordinary object and connect it to spiritual things. It is very important that the things that are taught in the classroom be mirrored in the home so the church and the home can work together in building a solid foundation.

New Beginnings

It is great for a church to plan and implement a Child Dedication service. Although this service can be held on the child's first day at church, many churches incorporate this special event as part of an annual "Mother's Day" service or an annual "Family Day" service.

The following is an example of a Baby Dedication service held at First Baptist Church in Nashville, Tennessee. Pastor Frank Lewis describes the services as follows...

I began the service by bringing the infant in from the back of the sanctuary. I walked toward the front of the sanctuary, making sure that everybody could see the baby. I was miked and I talked to the baby as I went.

I introduced the baby to his new church family. I talked about the responsibility this congregation has in providing an atmosphere that will be conductive to directing the child toward faith. Just as we were now walking up the aisle, one day this child would walk up this aisle on his own, come to this altar and publicly profess his faith in Jesus Christ.

Once I was at the front, I alerted the church that before we could blink an eye, this child would be sitting on this from pew, ready to celebrate his graduation, too. We had a responsibility between this day and that day to encourage this one toward faith.

The parents joined me at the front. I explained to the parents that their child's biblical name means _________________. While I still held the baby, I challenged them by saying "(Parents) do you vow to provide an atmosphere and spiritual nurturing that will incline your child's heart toward the gospel and a saving relationship with Jesus Christ?" I waited for them to respond.

I next challenged the church by saying, "Church family, do you take responsibility to assist this family as you teach and work with them in Sunday school, discipleship classes, RA's, Choirs, and in conversation in the hallway that will encourage them in spiritual development of their child? I waited for their response.

Then I huddled with the family and prayed with them for God's protection and guidance. The prayer closed as I lay my hands on the child and pronounced the following blessing: "By God's power, may you be wise, be strong, be pure.

The following day, I mailed a letter to the child, sealed in an envelope with instructions that it is to be opened on the child's 12th birthday.

Date of Dedication Service

Infant's Full Name
Street
Mailing Address City, State, ZIP

Dear ___________:

Happy Birthday! I am writing this greeting to you on the day of your Parent-Child Dedication at First Baptist Church, Nashville. As you read this letter, you are celebrating your 12th birthday. I hope today is a special day for you.

God blessed you with two very special parents. They prayed for you during your mother's pregnancy. Earlier today at your dedication, we reminded your parents of their responsibility to provide for you a home in which Christ is honored. We prayed that you would grow up learning God's love and that one day you would accept Jesus Christ as your personal Savior and Lord.

Now you are 12 years old. Your parents have made most of life's important decisions for you until now. There is one decision only you can make. You alone must decide how to respond to God's love for you in Jesus. If you have already received Jesus as your Savior, I pray that you will continue to grow as a Christian and that you will stay close to Jesus in the years ahead. If you have not yet received Jesus as Savior, I urge you to trust Him. This has been our prayer for many years.

May God bless you on this special birthday.

In Christ's Love,
Pastor's Name

Ministering To Children 2-3

"Self-Discoverers"

The day in the life of a child ages 2-3 could be described as being a 'whirlwind' of activity that keeps going and going! They are involved in constant activity from the time they wake up in the morning until bedtime. As they engage in activity, they will often do so on their own and away from the group. Give them a toy to play with and they will take the toy and play alone...doing their own thing, thus becoming 'self-discoverers'. The growth of these children is so rapid that one can tell differences in them from week to week. Their vocabulary will increase up to 300 words and they will begin piecing words together and begin using sentences. These children can follow simple directions and desires to help with activity.

Mentally, these children are learning the foundational basics of life. They are learning to follow directions, good eating habits, sleeping habit, bladder and bowel control, getting along with others and talking well. They are absorbing information like a sponge, making this a great time to lay the foundation for spiritual things. Because these children do not know how to read, they must depend on others to tell them truth. They fully trust those who care for them, making this a great opportunity and a responsibility to those who teach.

Children 2-3 years old have very short attention spans. This age group is often given the name "Terrible twos" because of the various things they may do making them 'typical children'. Bedwetting, tearing things up, making messes, getting in to things and becoming curious...are some of these that all children of this age encounter. These children are discoverers and are curious about the world around them. They greatly use their imagination and the concept of time is unknown to them. They often want things NOW and must learn how to wait.

These 'Self-Discoverers' learn best in and through the things they are very familiar with, especially home relationships. They see God as a personal being, therefore they understand that if mom and dad love and care for them, God also loves and cares for them. They want to be involved with and imitate their parent's everyday activities; folding clothes, gardening and using simple tools. Pets are meaningful to them whether their own or someone else's. They are interested in little babies and professions held in the community, such as firemen, policemen and postal workers.

Spiritually, they think of Jesus as a 'real' person and they want to express their love for him verbally. This is a great teaching time regarding prayer! They love to listen to Bible stories and learn fun things that they relate to. For example; Jesus was born as a little baby; He had parents; and Jesus grew up to be big and strong. Because they connect everything to home relationships and things they are familiar with, they love singing songs and learning about church, people and the Bible. They are ready to listen to short, simple Bible stories and react to them. Their interest in learning and curiosity in the world around them makes this a vital age for laying early foundations about God, church, the Bible and other spiritual things.

Theological Concepts of Children 2-3

About God	God loves me God takes care of me. God loves and cares for my family. God provides sun and rain. God does good for people. God is all about me. God wants me to talk with Him. God made the world God made me. I can praise God by singing and praying. I can tell God I am sorry for the bad things I do. I should please and obey God.
About Jesus	Jesus loves me. Jesus once lived on earth, but now is in heaven. Jesus is God's Son. Jesus is a Friend. Jesus said good things which are in the Bible. Jesus was once a child like me.
About the Bible	The Bible tells about God. The Bible is a good Book. The Bible is a special Book. I should love the Bible.
About Home and Parents	God gave parents. I should obey my parents.
About Church and Sunday school	Church is a place to learn about God. Church is a place to see friends. Church is God's house. I should like to go to church. I can give money to God's house to help buy things.

About Others	God gives grownups to care for me. Others may be good friends. Others may sometimes be unkind. Jesus wants me to be kind to others and share with them.
About Angels and Last Things	Angels came to tell people when Jesus was born Angels love God and praise Him.

What My Child Can Learn In the Classroom at Age 2-3

Because of what the child can understand about God, Jesus, the Bible and other information previously indicated, a child ages 2-3 can begin learning the following stories of the Bible. Although these children may not understand all of the concepts concerning each story, they can begin learning the basic important truths of each one, thus beginning a biblical foundation. As each child matures and truths are repeated with deeper meaning, the child understands on a greater level. The hope for this age group is to begin laying the foundational "stepping stones" of Bible knowledge with basic information about stories they can learn or relate to. Teachers and workers may use this as a checklist for teaching. This checklist can be used as a guideline for measuring appropriate teaching information.

In the Beginning	God's Creation	God Made the Animals
Adam & Eve	Garden of Eden	Cain & Abel
Noah & the Flood	Raindrops & Rainbows	Food for Elijah
10 Lepers	Zacchaeus	Jonah & the Whale
Baby Jesus	10 Commandments	Baby Moses
David & Goliath	Daniel & the Lions Den	Jesus loves Children (Mk 10)
Abraham & Isaac	Jesus as a little boy	John the Baptist
Teachings of Jesus	Jesus' Miracles	Paul
Paul & Silas	Jesus' Death	Jesus' Resurrection
David	Parables	Peter

Before the children leave your class room to be promoted to the next class, they should have been exposed to these stories. Even though they may not be able to understand and remember all of the facts about these stories, they should be able to;

*Recognize different sight words from the Bible such as "God", "Jesus", "love", "promise", "pray", "heaven", etc…

*Recognize that the Bible is truth and it is God speaking to us.

*Understand that God sent His Son, Jesus to die for us because He loves us

*Tell how we can obey God through every day actions; i.e.: sharing, caring, loving, helping, praying, etc…

*Express love to God and Jesus verbally

*Tell others about God's love

Connecting to the Bible

Now that we understand some of the characteristics of a child 2-3 and know what they can understand, let's make a connection in how they can effectively learn about spiritual things.

Previously, we learned that children of this age learn best through discovery. Setting good, solid habits in the basics of life helps them to establish a good foundation in physical, as well as spiritual things. Biblical foundations are best taught in relationship to what these children are familiar with; their home and family. This gives a new meaning to the phrase "Children are a parent's first curriculum."

The key word to remember when working with children ages 2-3 is *"self-discoverers"*. These children are curious about the world around them and will use their imaginations along with a variety of activities to help them learn. Around 2 years of age, the child will tend to be a 'loner', pulling away to play, getting lost in their own little world. As the child gets closer to three, they will become a more part of a group activity and participating with other children. Their attention spans are short, but take interest in imitating other adults and becoming involved with parent's everyday activities.

Separating this child from his mother may be difficult, therefore a room of activity must entice the child to come and take part. The classroom must be bright and colorful with a variety of opportunities for activities that allow children to sit and play, as well as space for lots of movement. Work stations that allow the child to imitate adult caregivers are necessary for imaginary play; kitchens with pots and pans for cooking; sinks for dishwashing; workbenches with simple tools; baby beds for playing with dolls; etc…are just a few items children love to play with. It's a great idea to have music playing in the room as well or an interaction DVD playing to help draw the children in to play.

When teaching children of this age, it is important for the worker to choose a one sentence phrase for the day, incorporating many activities and opportunities to support that phrase. Repetition is key for their learning. For example, the worker may choose the phase "Jesus loves me". Upon receiving the child, the worker may say to the child, "I am so glad you came to Sunday school today! Jesus loves me and you and wants us to learn about Him." The worker may connect the phrase "Jesus Loves Me" and verbally illustrates how He loves us through each thing that is done during class time; snack time, play time, story time, music time, etc…Some ways to verbalize this could include," Jesus loves me and gives me good friends." Or "Jesus loves me and provides a good snack for me" (don't forget to thank Jesus by offering a blessing!). The music selected for the day could be "Jesus Loves Me" or "Jesus Loves the Little Children of the World". The worker can teach children of this age by connecting one sentence phrases to activities carried out during class. Repetition and connection are vital and necessary to help these children learn solid, foundational truths. Picture cards, colors and picture books are a must for these children.

Following the class, it is important that the worker communicate with the parent regarding the lesson. Encourage parents to continue using the one sentence phase throughout the week in various activities with their child. Soon, the child will be able to respond with the phrase being taught. The worker may provide helpful information for the parent to take home that gives ideas and helpful suggestions on making the lesson carry over into the home. This is one way the church can support the home in Christian education.

The Church Supports the Home

It is very important that we take what we learn during Sunday school or church and encourage parents to make sure that those things take place in the home. *Communication* will be the key so that parents and caregivers may be aware of what is being taught in the classroom. Parents may not realize that the Christian Education of their children must carry over into the home.

Teachers must keep parents abreast of what is taught in the classroom and offer ways for them to continue teaching their children at home. For example, if the teacher is teaching a lesson on prayer, they may give parents suggestions for incorporating prayer at home to encourage application and continued learning. Another lesson may be "Jesus Loves Me", but children must have opportunities other than at church to make application and put Scripture into action. Teachers can give parents suggestions of how they can use typical day to day activities to discuss God's blessings and how Jesus loves us. Parents can teach children that Jesus loves us by providing the things that we need such as food, clothing, shelter, etc...

Notes to the Teacher

The child will see your class as a fun place to be. Don't use this time to 'house' children until church is over! Be strategic in teaching this age child by making a plan and then working the plan. Remember to select the phrase, and then illustrate it through the activities in the class.

Some implications to include when teaching these children include providing choices when selecting books and toys. Provide consistency in response to their behaviors. "I like the way you are sharing with Jesse". "You cannot tear the page in the book". Use teachable moments throughout your time with the children by making connection to the Bible. Remember to speak in terms these children can understand

It is very important to arrive early to pre-set your class for as many of the activities as possible. Pray for each student that will attend your class and create an atmosphere of readiness before each child arrives. Make sure follow up information is ready to be sent home with parents encouraging them to continue teaching God's Word through the things they are familiar with at home.

"And these words, which I command thee this day, shall be in thine heart."And thou shalt teach them diligently unto thy children and shalt talk of them when thou sittest in thine house, and when thou liest down and when thou risest up." —Deuteronomy 6:6-7

As a reminder, always be aware of safety hazards in the classroom. All electrical outlets must have safety inserts and should not be exposed for little fingers to have access. Throw away toys with missing pieces and discard toys with small pieces that could become a choking hazard. It is a good idea to take home small toys each week and disinfect them as they seem to find themselves on the floor and into children's mouths.

-7-

"Understanding the Blueprints of Preschoolers"

"And thou shalt teach them diligently unto thy children, and shall talk of them when thou sittest in thine house, and when thou walkest by the way, and when thou liest down, and when thou risest us." —Deuteronomy 6:7

Ministering to Children 4-5

"Imaginative"

"Wigglers", "imitators" and """energetic" are just a few words that describe the four and five year old child. This child finds himself no longer playing along side of a group, but actively participating in it. They are improving their fine motor skills and enjoy using crayons and pencils. Activity and energy is a learning advantage for these students and should never be discouraged.

The four and five year old child begins to learn about "friends" and begins to discover humor. Their fun-loving personalities often bring about loud, boisterous laughter as they spend a great deal of time being silly and discovering how to tell jokes. They enjoy singing simple songs, rhymes and nonsense words. They may use some bad words (if he/she has heard them spoken repeatedly) and may be susceptible to some discipline needs because their new use of words.

As the child's vocabulary increase, so does his/her understanding and awareness of the world around them. They are curious and the word "Why" becomes the most popular word in their vocabulary. Children at this age begin to understand concepts and can compare abstract ideas. These children are beginning to cross over from what is an idea into what is real. For example, up until now, they do not have a full understanding of words such as 'ago', in the 'past', etc...Now, they are able to begin to understand time. They become less aware of themselves and become more curious in the world around them. They have a strong desire to help, therefore simple chores can begin being taught such as setting the table and helping to fold simple laundry items such as towels.

The four-year old reaches some 'milestones' that include skipping and hopping on one foot. They may be able to catch a ball and zip, button and unsnap clothing. The five year old can balance themselves on one foot with their eyes closed, dresses themselves and can use scissors. The four and five-year old can say 1,500-2,000 words and put together 8 word sentences. Many of them can tell you their address and phone numbers and can be encouraged to discuss the "what if's" in situations and stories. Foundational things such as colors, shapes, sight words, sorting and identifying money are great educational tools for the teacher because these things lay a foundation for things to come.

Socially, the four and five year old child enjoys playing with other children. Some may be rather bossy and others may create imaginary playmates. They love conversation and may change the rules of a game as they are playing. They are eager to please other adults and usually have good manners. These children have a great number of fears and are often afraid of the dark and monsters. They may name call and 'tattle' quite often. They enjoy dramatic play and role playing, and often have difficulties separating make-believe and reality.

Teaching children of this age is best done simply through *'teachable moments'*. The teacher teaches the child through things and events using those very moments to teach them 'on the spot'. Because biblical foundations of these children are best learned through 'teachable moments', we *must* be aware of activity going on with the children in the classroom and be prepared to teach in and through those activities. For example, little Johnny does not want to share his toy with his friend in class and becomes very unkind. The teacher can tell little Johnny that Jesus is our Friend and He loves us and gives us things to play with. Jesus also gives us friends to play with. He wants us to share our things and be kind to our friends. The teacher can also teach the child how to apologize. A simple lesson on forgiveness can be taught here as well.

Another example of a teachable moment could be a child's mother brings treats for all of the children in the class to have at snack time. Before having snack, the teacher can express to the children that little Susie's mom loves them and has sent a special snack. Before having the snack, the teacher may offer a prayer of thanks for friends that loves us and gives us special gifts. The students may express their thanks to Susie's mom by sending pictures they had drawn or saying "Thank You" as a group when picking up Susie.

Theological Concepts of Children 4-5 Years Old

About God	God loves me and others.
	God cares for all who love Him
	God cares for and loves families
	God made all things
	God is to be trusted and depended on
	God is everywhere
	God will hear prayer anytime
	God sent Jesus to die for sin
	God wants me to be thankful for all He has made
	God wants me to obey Him by obeying my parents
	God loves me
About Jesus	Jesus loves me and is my best friend
	Jesus came to be the Savior
	Jesus is now living in Heaven
	Jesus will help me to obey and share
	Jesus wants all children to love Him
	Jesus is always with me
	Jesus died for me
	Jesus can help me do hard things

About the Bible	The Bible tells about God The Bible is God's Word God tells me what He wants me to do in the Bible The Bible helps me know what to do The Bible is a Book of true stories
About Home and Parents	God gave parents to care for me and teach me God gave parents to pray for me I should obey my parents I should want to love and please my parents I sin when I disobey my parents or am unkind
About Church and Sunday School	Church is a place to learn, sing, and worship God Church is a place to meet with others who love God Church is a special place Church is a place where we learn about God
About Others	God made all people God loves everyone and wants all to love Him God wants me to tell others about Jesus Others may not share as I do Others may be loving and kind to me I am to be kind, share and pray for others God wants me to share my money God wants people to help others
About Angels and Last Things	Some angels are good and some are bad Satan is a bad angel who did not want to please God Satan and his angels want us to do bad things.

What My Child Can Learn In the Classroom at Age 4-5

Because of what a child can understand about God, Jesus, the Bible and other information previously indicated, a child ages 4-5 can learn the following stories in the Bible. Many of these are stories may have been introduced previously, but can be repeated with a deeper level of understanding. They may not have a full scope of each of these stories, but may have some knowledge concerning each of them. For example, they may not know all of the events in David's life, but they do know he killed a giant. Repetition is a vital element in learning, especially when a story is repeated and presented from different perspectives.

In the Beginning	Adam & Eve	The Garden of Eden
Cain & Abel	Noah & the Flood	The Tower of Babel
Abraham & Sarah	Abraham & Isaac	Hagar & Ishmael
Food for Elijah	10 Lepers	Zacchaeus
Jonah & the Whale	Baby Moses	The Burning Bush
Crossing the Red Sea	10 Commandments	The Golden Calf
The Tabernacle	Cloud & the Fire	Twelve Spies
Wandering in the Wilderness		Samson & Delilah
Hannah	Samuel	David & Goliath
Elijah & the Widow	12 Disciples	Elijah & Prophets of Baal
Elijah Raises Boy from the Dead		Job
Jesus is Born	Jesus As A Boy	Daniel & the Lions Den
The Fiery Furnace	Jonah & the Whale	John the Baptist
Jesus Tempted	Fishers of Men	Friend Through the Roof
Jesus Heals a Cripple	Pool At Bethesda	Jesus Calms A Storm
Jairus Daughter	Feeding of 5,000	Peter Walking on Water
Jesus & the Children	Jesus Heals Blind Man	Lazarus
Good Samaritan	Mary & Martha	Prodigal Son
Blind Bartimaeus	Widow's Mite	Judas
Jesus is Crucified	Jesus is Risen	Visiting the Tomb
Doubting Thomas	Disciples Fishing	Jesus Goes Up in the Clouds
Peter & John	Paul & Silas	Fruits of the Spirit

Remember it is very important that we teach in ways that children will understand. It is important that use words in "literal" terms because children believe what we actually say. Avoid using slang words or symbols for children to gain true meaning to what we are teaching.

Also, relate the story to something they are familiar with. They can relate to things that deal with family, friends, playing and feelings such as being happy and sad. Application of these stories takes place when children can see themselves, their families, their friends, etc…in the story.

Connecting to the Bible

Now that we understand the development of children ages 4-5, let's make a connection in how they can effectively learn about spiritual things.

Previously, we learned that children of this age can be best ministered to by simply using 'teachable moments'. Using activities and situations the child is currently involved in to teach Bible 'truths' will build solid spiritual foundations. These children are beginning to understand right from wrong for themselves and others. They can be assured in what the Bible says about certain actions and how Jesus wants us to respond. Another key word is *repetition*. Workers will find themselves repeating these truths over and over until the child eventually begins to learn them in their heart. Although we may teach these children in various situations and various events, we are still teaching many of the same truths that we want them to carry out for a lifetime.

The attention span of the four and five year old is about five to ten minutes. When teaching Bible stories, we must keep them simple and without detailed information. It is best to follow up a 'still' activity with a 'moving' activity to help support what you have just taught them. For example, the teacher may teach a short lesson on Noah's Ark. Following the story, the teacher may roll out long sheets of white paper and have the students to draw some of the animals that were on the ark. The teacher may have songs playing on a CD player such as "Arky, Arky" and "Who Built the Ark?" while the students draw with crayons and pencils. The snack that day could be animal crackers or cookies!

The four and five year old child is separating reality with make-believe. The Bible and the things about God and Jesus should be reinforced as 'real' and should be taught as truth repetitively. These children also believe what you tell them literally, so workers must be careful with their use of words. For example, "Asking Jesus into your heart" may mean to a four and five year old physically putting Jesus inside their body.

I heard a story one day about a teacher who taught a Sunday school class of four and five year olds using the story of Adam and Eve. She explained to the students that Adam and Eve were driven out of the Garden of Eden. She asked the class to draw a picture about the story they had just learned. When the teacher came around to see the student's art work, she noticed that one of the students had drawn a picture of a car with a man in the driver's seat and a man and a woman in the back seat. When the teacher asked the student to explain his picture, he said that it was a picture of Jesus driving Adam and Eve out of the Garden of Eden!

Another story was told about a student in the class whose niece was expecting a baby. The teacher explained that when the baby was born, the student would become an aunt. Without saying a word, the student went away in fear thinking she was going to turn into a bug! (an ant, not an aunt!) This child did not realize the difference until the child was born and she truly became an aunt and not an ant!

Another great idea when teaching children of this age is open discussion after the Bible story with "what if". For example, "What if God hadn't sent the rain?" or "What if Jesus would have never been born?" This allows the children to think about story possibilities and allows the teacher to reinforce God's purpose in why He chose to do what He did.

When asking the children to respond to lessons previously taught, or when reviewing memory verses, always ask questions allowing them to fill in the blanks. The teacher should give a pause, allowing them to recall what they have learned. As the students respond, the teacher can gain an understanding of what they have learned and clear up any wrong thinking they may have. Asking questions that require more than a yes or a no answer causes the children to think and gives the class an opportunity for discussion.

The Church Supports the Home

It is important that the home reinforce what is being done at the church. Many times this doesn't happen in the home because parents simply don't know what needs to be done. The four and five year old is continuing to learn many foundational things. Many of these foundational things at this age deal with their emotions and social skills. These children need to be taught about right and wrong behaviors and parents need to use day to day activities and situations to teach them about sharing, caring, loving, helping and understanding. Parents must be made aware of 'teachable moments' at home and in the community. Parents can use these moments to teach their children about the world around them.

Other times parents can teach their child in "teachable moments"

*On the way home from the grocery store, the parent may say, "Look at all of this food that God has blessed us with! There are many boys and girls who do not have the food that we have." Praise the Lord verbally for giving you food to eat! You are teaching praise.
*Another time is at Christmas time and the gifts that are given to us. Let them also understand that Christmas is not about presents, but the gift of a baby named Jesus who was born to save the world. You are teaching true meaning.
*Your child gets together with a group of friends and one of the children is being unkind. Stop and talk to the group about being kind to one another and loving one another with our words. You are teaching kindness.
*When our children use different emotions such as jealousy, anger, sadness, etc…You are teaching control in our emotions.
*Your child has two of one kind of toy. You may suggest they give one of the toys to a friend at church or preschool who may not have that toy. You are teaching giving
*Visiting a child who is not feeling well. You are teaching caring.

The list goes on and on because learning doesn't stop! When children begin learning through these teachable moments, it is carried over into other parts of their lives and is continued throughout their lifetime. Parents must understand that children learn in their daily experiences.

Notes to the Teacher

The key word for teachers of fours and fives is to *observe* what is going on in the classroom. Don't miss the MANY 'teachable moments' that will take place inside the classroom. Plan the lesson, provide the activities that will support the lesson and teach in and through these teachable moments. *Watch* for these opportunities to come about and *strike* while the iron is hot! *Be prepared* to turn situations and activities into meaningful learning times by connecting it to the Bible and spiritual truths. Provide helpful information to parents about some of these opportunities.

-8-

"Understanding the Blueprints of Elementary Students"

"I love them that love me; and those that seek me early shall find me."
—Proverbs 8:17

Ministering to Children Ages 6-7

"Transition"

Children between the ages of 6-7 learn more by doing than by observing. Instead of watching the teacher demonstrating something to a class, they'd rather be a part of it. Children of this age are very teachable and get excited about learning. They are full of movement and should have plenty of opportunity to do so.

The six and seven year old is beginning a time of "transition". They are leaving their preschool years behind and stepping out into a much bigger world. He is striving for acceptance and approval from teachers and parents. They can feel insecure and left out if criticized. They still want the love and support they receive from home, but are ready to step out and take on new challenges. These first and second grade students are beginning to step into yet another phase of the developmental process which includes foundational and educational learning. The six and seven year old loves to copy adults, repeating what they hear and imitating what they see. This is often reflected when they are *pretend* playing doing household chores or taking care of their dolls. Their vocabulary doubles; they can begin to understand time and learns better through a variety of activities and experiences.

Physically, the six and seven year old child is very active! They enjoy many activities and stay busy. They are constantly tapping their toe, twisting in their chairs or humming. These children love movement and find it very difficult to keep still. These children love to paint, draw, jump rope, build things and ride their bikes. Although their attention span is still relatively short, they must learn to listen more closely and follow directions. They are also able to adapt to a more structured environment. As they mature, they will be able to sit for longer periods of time and follow more detailed instruction. It is important that they learn and demonstrate these important rules now or they will miss out on learning many foundational truths. The six year old will begin to lose their 'baby' teeth, tie their shoes, begin reading and writing and learn the value of numbers. The seven year old will learn the same, but can understand on a much deeper level.

Socially, these children are learning to get along. They are learning to share with others, while realizing that the world is not all about them. They love group activities and love to compete with others! They like to play alone, but friends are becoming important to them. The six and seven year old develops *best friends* and *enemies.* They are jealous of friends and siblings, and enjoy playing with friends of the same gender.

Mentally, they have a difficult time differentiating between reality and fantasy. Parents and teachers must be clear in teaching these children so that children will not enter into wrong thinking. Parents and teachers must communicate these differences to these children and help them to understand what is real and what is not. These children are often influenced by adults, therefore what they see adults do will be perceived as right. Whatever the adult says to them will be received as 'truth' and their trust in adults is very high.

Spiritually, the six and seven year old will begin to understand many biblical truths, especially if they have been in church most of their lives. If so, many children of this age receive Christ as their Savior and begin their simple walk as a Christian. Many parents fear that their children take this step without truly 'understanding' what has happened to them. Because we can't see inside their hearts and know what they understand, parents and teachers must ask these children questions and allow them to respond. When the child can respond with correct answers to questions such as "What is sin?" and "Why Jesus died on a cross", we can be assured they have realized what the plan of salvation is. Children of this age are easy to accept Christ because of their simple faith. Matthew 19 says *"Suffer the little children to come unto Me for such is the kingdom of God."* We must be careful in leading a child of this age to Christ without having them to do something they do not understand. When parents and teachers are unsure about what has taken place in a child's life, they must pray and seek God to show them.

Children of this age enjoy reading. What a wonderful time to have children exposed to good Bible story books! Their new gained desire to read will open the opportunity to encourage them to read about characters (kids just like them) in the Bible and about other spiritual things. These children love to tell stories and hear stories. They are ready to learn basic truths about the Bible on their level. The six and seven year old can begin to connect stories to their own personal lives and make application.

Theological Concepts of Children 6-7 Years Old

About God	God loves me and my family and my friends God loves all the people of the world. God wants people to love Him too. God wants people to give their lives to Him. God provides food for people by letting plants grow. God takes care of the world He made. God is good, but He is also against evil. God wants us to pray and read our Bible. God is holy and cannot fail. God has all power to help me.
About Jesus	Jesus is the Son of God. Jesus came to earth to die for sin. Jesus wants us to accept Him as our personal Savior. Jesus wants to help people go to God.

	Jesus wants to take sin from our lives. Jesus never did anything wrong. Jesus rose from the dead and now lives in heaven. Jesus loves us and wants to e our friend. Jesus did many wonderful miracles while on earth. Jesus can help me choose to do the rights things.
About the Bible	The Bible is God's Book, for it tells about Him The Bible tells us what God wants. The Bible tells how God worked with others. The Bible tells much about us. The Bible is a good Book to study, for it helps us. The Bible should be read and memorized. The Bible contains sixty-six books. The Bible has two major parts, called the Old and New Testaments.
About Home and Parents	Parents are God's leaders for us on earth. Parents want to help us, so we should obey them. Parents love us, so we should love them too. Parents provide food and clothing and home for us. God is an important guest in our home at all times.
About Church and Sunday School	Church is God's house. Church is a place where God's people go. Church is a happy place. Church is a place for songs, prayer and Bible study. Church needs out help to keep it clean and quiet. Church is not just a building but also the people in it. I can give to the Lord's work through the church.
About Others	Others may want the same thing I do; I must share. Others may not want to do the same thing I do; I must learn to give in halfway. Others may need something very much; I must learn to give. Others may be in trouble; I must learn to pray. Others may be unkind; I must learn to forgive. Others may not know Jesus; I must learn to tell about Him.

About Angels and Last Things	Satan tempts us to sin and disobey God. Good angels worship and praise God. Good angels are God's servants. Jesus has gone to heaven to prepare a place there for all who love Him. Jesus is coming to take us to live with Him forever.

What a Child Can Learn in the Classroom at Age 6-7

The 6-7 year old child can read simple passages from the Bible. They love to learn and tell simple Bible stories and enjoys acting them out for others. This student is developing 'reasoning skills" and will ask many questions to understand what is being taught. Teachers must make sure that wrong thoughts and perceptions are corrected so that students understand true understanding. Because of what the child can understand about God, Jesus, the Bible and other information previously indicated, a child ages 6-7 can learn the following stories. Many of these stories are repeated because as children mature and are able to understand more concepts, they can learn a deeper meaning about each story. These children have an "if Jesus said it, then I believe it" attitude and will accept what you say as Truth. Remember, we are building foundations, while biblical and spiritual knowledge is obtained. As children mature and get older, the goal is to build stronger, more solid foundations. As they receive greater knowledge and inspiration, greater understanding motivates them to personally allow application to take place with each story that is learned.

In the Beginning	Adam & Eve	The Garden of Eden
Cain & Abel	Noah & the Flood	The Tower of Babel
Abraham & Sarah	Abraham & Isaac	Hagar & Ishmael
Food for Elijah	10 Lepers	Zacchaeus
Jonah & the Whale	Baby Moses	The Burning Bush
Crossing the Red Sea	10 Commandments	The Golden Calf
The Tabernacle	Cloud & the Fire	Twelve Spies
Wandering in the Wilderness		Samson & Delilah
Hannah	Samuel	David & Goliath
Elijah & the Widow	12 Disciples	Elijah & Prophets of Baal
Elijah Raises Boy from the Dead		Job

Jesus is Born	Jesus As A Boy	Daniel & the Lions Den
The Fiery Furnace	Jonah & the Whale	John the Baptist
Jesus Tempted	Fishers of Men	Friend Through the Roof
Jesus Heals a Cripple	Pool At Bethesda	Jesus Calms A Storm
Jairus Daughter	Feeding of 5,000	Peter Walking on Water
Jesus & the Children	Jesus Heals Blind Man	Lazarus
Good Samaritan	Mary & Martha	Prodigal Son
Blind Bartimaeus	Widow's Mite	Judas Friends: Jonathan & David
Jesus is Crucified	Jesus is Risen	Visiting the Tomb
Doubting Thomas	Disciples Fishing	Jesus Goes Into the Clouds
Peter & John	Paul & Silas	Fruits of the Spirit

Connecting to the Bible

Now that we understand the development of children ages 6-7, let's connect that with how they can effectively learn about spiritual things.

We learned that children of this age are in transition. Although they still display many of the characteristics of a younger child, they are now taking the steps toward more mature learning. The six year old student must learn to adapt to learning in a classroom situation, while the seven year old must learn to adapt to longer periods of sitting still and listening. It is *very* important that students learn to develop good listening skills and are able to follow directions so that many biblical truths can be taught. The teacher must develop ways to have them to respond to biblical knowledge so they can correct any wrong thinking. When students are not listening, they may miss important truths being taught in the Sunday school. Teachers must also incorporate some "hands-on" activities to allow lessons to "come to life" for the student. Remember, these students much rather be a part of the lesson than merely listening to it. As the lessons come *alive*, students of this age will begin to personally connect with what is being taught with their own personal life. If they are taught a story in the Bible of a child their age, they begin to see themselves in the shoes of that child. If the family of this child is discussed, they begin to think of themselves and their families in the same situation. The Bible will begin to become a Book of *real* stories about *real* people who are just like them.

Teaching needs to be alternated with activity, therefore "hands on" learning must take place. Following the lesson, the teacher may lead the students in a game that will support what they have just been taught. These children love competition, so the teacher may divide them into teams and let them play against each other. Another great way to give students a "hands-on" experience is to allow them to become a part of the culture of the story being taught by allowing them to dress in some of these biblical costumes or prepare some of the foods they may have eaten. The experience of being in the setting of the story will broaden their appreciation of the event and make learning more fun.

Friendships are developed and become very important to the six and seven year old. They take on "best friends" and learn the ins and outs of getting along with others. Through their friendships, they experience many emotions such as jealousy and envy, while learning to love and give. This also includes their relationships with their brothers and sisters. What an awesome time to teach about friendships in the Bible! Not only can we teach stories about friendships and sibling found in the Bible, but we can also teach about how to be a friend and what value friendships have for us. In I Samuel 20, we read about a friendship between Jonathan and David. Luke 5 tells a story of a paralytic man who was brought to Jesus by his friends because they had faith that their friend could be healed. Stories such as these not only give us accounts of what happened and how God helped them, but give us examples on how to handle similar situations in our own personal life. The Bible is a compilation of stories and events just like situations we go through today. We can learn from those in God's Word who have already experienced what we are going through and learn from them. If God did these things for those in the Bible, surely He will do the same for us!

The six and seven year old student loves to read! This is a great opportunity to encourage them to read the Bible and other good Christian material. The teacher should encourage the students to bring their Bible to the Sunday school class. These children can be taught how to write a chapter and verse such as John 3:16 (The three meaning the third chapter and sixteen meaning the number of the verse). Students can learn important information about the Bible such as the Bible is divided into two main sections; the Old Testament and the New Testament; written by over 40 men over a period of about 1,600 years, etc…They should begin learning to look up Bible verses where familiar Scripture and stories can be found. The six and year old can gain good experience in looking up Scripture by giving questions and allowing them to look up the answers.

The Church Supports the Home

The six and seven year old child is developing such a foundation for learning that carry over *must* be take place at home. Not only does this help the student to remember the information taught in class, but reinforces how important that it by being communicated by the parents. These children are full of questions and desire to know more about EVERYTHING!

Earlier we learned that these "transition" students learn more by doing than observing. Encourage the parents to allow their children to take an active part in "spiritual" things at home. For example; let the child say the blessing over the food or say prayers at bedtime. As they are learning about prayer from God's Word, they are able to experience it by doing it at home. Another way is to begin family devotions. Encourage the parents to let their children read Scripture, lead in prayer or offer prayer requests during these gatherings. As a family, parents can provide opportunities and allow their child to become an active participant in ministry such as; preparing a dish together and taking it to an elderly person in the church. Actions such as these allow them to learn by doing and it reinforces what is being taught in the church.

Structure is necessary for the six and seven year old. Encourage the parents to develop and maintain some sort of schedule when it comes to day to day activities. Children need structure and should learn to include a variety of activities in their day. A schedule that involves doing homework, play time and a time to be with God are all an important elements that should be included. As children develop healthy habits in maintaining a schedule, they learn to make time for the most important things, while never neglecting the necessary things for living. Teaching children how to do this now will help them in maintaining their schedules as they get older and take on more responsibility.

Earlier in this chapter, we discussed how children are influenced by adults, therefore what they see adults do will be perceived as right. Parents should realize how important their witness is to their very own children. Children should see their parents displaying the same values and behaviors as they would at church. They should walk the walk and talk the talk. If children see their parents as something different, this teaches their children that you can go to church on Sunday and do whatever you want throughout the week and its okay. What they see is what they will eventually do. Talk with parents about the image they reflect to their children.

Notes to the Teacher

The key words to remember when teaching this age is *foundation* and *doers*. Learning how to be good listeners and following directions will help develop good learning habits that will follow them from this point forward. Do not only teach them the Word of God, but show them how to take action in it. Provide opportunities for these children to participate in activities that are not only carried out in the classroom but at home. Encourage the parents of these children to take action on what is being taught by given them examples of ideas to carry out at home

The six and seven year old is setting the foundation for future learning. Now is the time to begin to teach them some Bible basics. They are ready to learn basic Bible knowledge and can do so in some really fun ways! Acting out stories with costumes, riddles, Bible games, charades, and group activities are just some ways to have fun and learn at the same time! The Books of the Bible, the Twelve Disciples, the Fruits of the Spirit and the Ten Commandments are just some of the things that should be taught. Here are just a couple of fun ways to teach children the Books of the Bible:

Wrap cereal boxes in brown paper and write a book of the Bible on the edge of the box. Divide the class into two teams. Put the boxes in order showing the names of the books of the Bible. Have the children to turn with their backs toward the boxes and remove one of the boxes. Ask the children to turn around and identify the book that is missing. For a more difficult challenge, mix all of the boxes up and have the students put the books in order. To make it *really* challenging, make two sets of Books of the Bible and make it a team competition. See which team can put them in correct order first!

If you are unable to do this activity with cereal boxes, a simpler version is using index cards. Make two sets of index cards with one book of the Bible if each card. Mix them up and turn them upside down. Divide the class into two teams. The first person chooses the top card from the stack and runs to the other end of the class and places the card in the correct sequence. When they return to the line, the next person goes. The team that completes all 66 Books of the Bible in the correct order wins! This same game can be done with the Twelve Disciples, Fruits of the Spirit and the Ten Commandments. We see it as learning...Children see it as fun!

Ministering to Children 8-9

"Middlers"

"Care-free", "Doers" and "expressive" are best words to describe the child ages 8-9. Children of this age are often referred to as *middlers* because they are in the middle of their childhood. At school, these children are 3rd and 4th grade students who are enjoying life, while discovering themselves individually. Their frustration level is at an all time low, while their self-esteem is at all time high. They are not afraid to try new things and want to "do it all"!

Physically, boys and girls are about equal in their ability to play sports. As they age, boys will gain better large muscle movement and girls will develop better small muscle movements. Large muscle movements in boys naturally lead them to play sports, while small muscle movements allow girls to become better at being able to do cursive writing and playing piano.

Socially, these students tend to play better as a group for longer periods of time than in their younger years. Although they prefer activities with their own sex, the older middler becomes interested in boy-girl relationships, but often doesn't admit it. "Middlers" enjoy friendships with others, while taking on more "best friends". They enjoy spending time with their peers and want to get to know them better. Approval and acceptance of parents and other adults are important to them and will go above and beyond to make it happen. They have a strong need to *"belong"* and should be a part of activities in which they can participate and contribute. Role models and "hero's" are important in the lives of these students, making it ultimately necessary that we surround these children with good examples and godly influences.

These students are taking more steps toward "growing up" and are able to spend more time away from home, even several days, without getting homesick. For the 8-9 year old child, parents and family are still the most influential and they still desire participating in activities with them. Because they are no longer a baby and wants to be treated as such, parents must save hugs and kisses for private times. Middlers are developing their personal uniqueness as they discover their personal likes and dislikes. They are learning who they are and what special qualities they possess within themselves. There are no two students "alike" and should be "affirmed" for their own special qualities and abilities individually. They need to feel accepted and worthwhile as individual because of who they are and how God has made them.

The third and fourth grader enjoys reading and desires opportunities to express themselves. They develop a sense of humor and love to tell jokes! They have learned how to do 'cursive' writing, which opens great opportunity for student to write their feelings down on paper and express themselves while perfecting this new skill. They are learning to do fractions and enjoy reading, drawing and painting. Emotionally, these students are learning to handle feelings and may experience 'outburst' which result in tears, anger and overexcitement.

The 8-9 year old is interested in spiritual things. They want to know about God and experience personal closeness with Him. They want to pray more and accept all that God says in His Word. There is nothing gray to this student…it's black or white, right or wrong. These students begin to learn about guilt, which may ultimately lead them to accept salvation. They enjoy learning more about God and the Bible, and are ready to grasp deeper spiritual concepts. They are curious about "death" and realize there are two spirit worlds. The middler enjoys creating and participating in spontaneous worship.

Mentally, they are able to think concretely. They realize that some things are not "literal" in their meaning and can grasp symbolic interpretation. The 8-9 year old student can begin to think logically and symbolically. Middlers are "multitaskers" and must learn to think in a 'step' process. The student has to learn or accomplish one step before going on to the next. As each step is learned, students must be given opportunities to use and expand what they have learned before moving on to the next step. These students can understand "reversibility" which means the student can retrace the steps to solve a problem or reverse the sequence to begin at the start again. For example; a child can learn that they can count to 10 by counting 1,2,3,4,5,6,7,8,9,10. They can also start at 10 and count backwards to begin at the same place in which they began. The same works with mathematical problems in addition or subtraction.

Workers of this age group may be more of a "guider" than a teacher of knowledge. Because these students are exciting about learning and doing, the teacher must continually guide students as they learn more about God, while correcting any misconceptions they may have learned along the way. The teacher must also use a great deal of time listening to their students and directing them to discovering their special gifts and talents God has given them.

Theological Concepts of Children Ages 8-9

About God	God is all powerful, and wise, and everywhere. God is present with me at all times. God wants to help me as I grow. God loves me and wants me to love God. God made the universe and all in it. God wants me to pray each day. God always answers prayers with yes, no or wait. God loves people all over the world. God the Holy Spirit is a person who is spirit. When I receive Christ as my Savior, the Holy Spirit comes into my life.
About Jesus	Jesus is the Son of God, the Savior. Jesus died on the cross for sin. Jesus can give salvation to those who ask. Jesus can forgive sin. Jesus loves me even when I sin. Jesus wants me to be a disciple and follow Him.

About the Bible	The Bible is an exciting Book to read. The Bible is a true Book, not fiction. The Bible is God's Word. The Bible should be read each day. The Bible has many important verses to be memorized. The Bible is God's Truth. The Bible tells what God wants us to know.
About Home and Parents	Parents have rules for me to follow, but they also have God's rules to follow. Parents are to me what God is to my parents. Parents want me to be a part of the family group. Home is a secure place where I can find my strength. Home is a happy place. Home is a place where I can talk over my problems with my parents. Home is a place where I can learn to follow rules.
About Church and Sunday School	Church is like a school, except that I learn about God and the Bible. Church is a place where I can worship God. Church is a place to sing about God. Church is a place for families. Church is a happy place where I want to go. Church needs my help to be all that it should.
About Others	Others include a wider world, far beyond the community. Others include foreign boys and girls across the sea. Others need help, which I can give. Others need the gospel, which I can share. Others need my prayers. Others need my money, which I can give.
About Angels and Last Things	Satan is a beautiful angel who sinned against God. Satan is the mot wicked of all created beings. Satan tempts Christians and leads them astray. Good angels protect God's people. Good angels are God's messengers to people and carry out God's judgments.

Heaven is for those who have accepted Christ as their personal Savior.

People who do not accept Christ as their Savior will be separated from God forever.

What A Child Can Learn At 8-9 Years Old

In the Beginning	Adam & Eve	The Garden of Eden
Cain & Abel	Noah & the Flood	The Tower of Babel
Abraham & Sarah	Abraham & Isaac	Hagar & Ishmael
Food for Elijah	10 Lepers	Zacchaeus
Jonah & the Whale	Baby Moses	The Burning Bush
Crossing the Red Sea	10 Commandments	The Golden Calf
The Tabernacle	Cloud & the Fire	Twelve Spies
Wandering in the Wilderness		Samson & Delilah
Hannah	Samuel	David & Goliath
Elijah & the Widow	12 Disciples	Elijah & Prophets of Baal
Elijah Raises Boy from the Dead		Job
Jesus is Born	Jesus As A Boy	Daniel & the Lions Den
The Fiery Furnace	Jonah & the Whale	John the Baptist
Jesus Tempted	Fishers of Men	Friend Through the Roof
Jesus Heals a Cripple	Pool At Bethesda	Jesus Calms A Storm
Jairus Daughter	Feeding of 5,000	Peter Walking on Water
Jesus & the Children	Jesus Heals Blind Man	Lazarus
Good Samaritan	Mary & Martha	Prodigal Son
Blind Bartimaeus	Widow's Mite Judas	Friends: Jonathan & David
Jesus is Crucified	Jesus is Risen	Visiting the Tomb
Doubting Thomas	Disciples Fishing	Jesus Goes Up In the Clouds
Peter & John	Paul & Silas	Fruits of the Spirit

If you will notice, this is a repeat of previous grades. Remember the difference when teaching students is that you deepen the message or teach it differently with each grade. For the 8-9 year old, we learned that they enjoy reading and their new found skill of "cursive" writing, therefore a great way to teach these students is to read the story to them and then have them creatively summarize the story by writing about it! We realized that these students '*worship*' or *idolized* heroes. Why not introduce them to a few from the Bible! Do a character study in which the students choose a character and write his biography? Any characters would work, but if you have never done this before, you may want to choose children from the Bible first. These students like to read about kids just like them and what they did for God. After experimenting with your students doing research on kids in the Bible, then they'll be more excited about doing some research on adults.

Would you really like to add a very creative flare to teaching? Choose a story from the Bible and have the students to do as much research about it as possible and write a narrative about the story. Have the students to gather costumes, props, etc…to build a scene that will depict the story. Have the class to 'still pose' as characters of the story as the narrative is being read. After practicing your story a few times, invite other classes to come and see what you've learned. It's exciting watching your class teach others about different stories and characters of the Bible!

Put the students' creative ability and need for expression to use by putting together "Bible Journals" for the class. At the end of each class time, give the students a few minutes to write down their feelings and comments about what they have learned that day. Keep the journals in your classroom so that students may write in them each week. The teacher can learn much about the student by reading their entries each week. Pray for each of these students individually while reading their hearts.

Connecting to the Bible

Now that we understand some of the characteristics of a child ages 8-9 and know what they can understand, let's make a connection in how they can effectively learn about spiritual things.

Children of this age will learn better through *expression* and *experience*. As we have learned, these children are excited about learning and are willing to try new things, opening themselves up to new experiences. They are expressive and want to their share their feelings, along with their new ability to do "cursive writing", so they must have opportunities to do just that. What a great time to teach these children about journaling! Journaling is not only a time to encourage them to jot down their thoughts, but to also write their prayers to God! Students can learn to pray for others and learn that it's just not about "me". Encourage them to write in their journals everyday and look back to see how God is working in their lives and in the lives of others! Other opportunities to use their writing abilities include allowing them to write answers on the chalkboard or fill in blanks to questions given to them on hand outs about their lesson.

"Middlers" loves to express themselves. Self expression can take place through writing their feeling on paper. These students can learn to express themselves through poetry and songs. This is a great opportunity to introduce them to the book of Psalms and the writings of David! Allow the students to express themselves to God just like David did! How about making greeting cards with Scripture and sending them to those who are sick in your community? These students also love writing notes of encouragement to those in the class or in your church to help lift their spirits.

Another great way for students in the 3rd and 4th grade to learn is to simply learn through creative experiences. For children of this age to "live in the present", past events must be brought up to where they are today. What better way to help them understand those in the Bible than to 'become' that character. Acting out stories, with biblical costumes will help them better understand the events of those they are studying and allows them to experience what is taking place.

Middlers have a strong need to belong and should be encouraged to participate in clubs and group activities. While many of them enjoy taking part in them, they also like to form and create clubs. Why not create a "Bible Club" for the students in your class. The purpose of a "Bible Club" could be to know as much about the Bible as possible! The what, where's and how's can be worked out together as a class and could prove to be a real motivator in helping them to learn Bible knowledge! How about participating in class projects such as a community clean up day or having the class to visit the nursing home or to do a project for one of the senior citizens in the church. These students also enjoy seeing how other students just like them make or do something of interest. Keep your students informed about how other children are making a difference to encourage them to get involved in making a difference as well.

These students love to participate! They want to be given more responsibility and are willing to take every opportunity to do so! Allow students to become actively involved in preparing for the class! Allow them to help you teach the lesson by assigning them special parts of the lesson to teach to the class. With time and guidance, we could spark an interest in others wanting to be future Sunday school teachers!

Memorizing is easy for the 8 & 9 year old. They enjoy reading and memorizing Scripture, while enjoying a little competition with it! Workers must remember that memorizing is not always learning. We must make sure that they understand or they are merely memorizing words. One way to determine if they understand Scripture they are memorizing would be to teach them about "paraphrasing". Paraphrasing is allowing the students to repeat what the Scripture is saying in their own words. If the student does not respond correctly, this allows the teacher to clear up misconceptions and helps them to understand its true meaning.

This student is now able to recall what the lesson was about the week before; therefore it is important for teachers to give review periodically. Take a few moments at the beginning of class to review what happened in the last class and have students to recall what they had learned. This review can be done by having them fill in blanks with missing words as you help them recall verbally or give them statements about the previous lesson allowing them to tell you if they are true or false. If answered incorrectly, this is your chance to correct them. This is also a great opportunity to expand what they've learned and to develop deeper Bible study skills. This can be done by reading Bible stories or simple Scripture and allowing them to draw different conclusions and outcomes. Allow the students to look at the "what ifs" and draw conclusions from hints or clues found in the story or Scripture.

"Hero Worship" is common among these students. Middlers recognize leaders and want to be just like them! Sometimes this "idolizing" can be so strong that the student wants to act like them, dress like them and mirror everything about them! Sports figures, pop music sensations and other public icons make tremendous impression on our students! Is it wrong for this to happen? Not as long as they are not enticed to do something that would ultimately lead them into sin or create a bad example or poor Christian witness. What an awesome time for students to look at Jesus Christ as their "Hero" or take Bible characters and look to them as examples in their lives! We need heroes such as Noah, Abraham, Jacob, Moses and others who remained faithful to God. How about personal heroes that can be found under the roofs of our own homes or under the roofs of the local church? Christian heroes found in the church such as Sunday school teachers, music directors, deacons and other lay leaders. We should not have the student to "worship" these individuals, but use the lives of these people to mirror examples of living a Godly life and being faithful to God.

One of the biggest tasks a teacher of 3rd and 4th graders is to help students discover their individual uniqueness. As they sort through their feelings, we must listen to them and let them know we care about them and want to help them. Students need teachers to be good listeners. The teacher will learn many things about the student *inside* the classroom, but they will learn much about the student *outside* the classroom. Personally get to know those you teach. Who are their friends? What are their parents like? How well do they do academically at school? What is their family like? Do they play sports? Play a musical instrument? What interests them? As the teacher begins to stop and listen to their students, they can find out a lot about those they teach. As the teacher begins to see their students as unique individuals, they can help guide them in being the best they can for Christ.

More children of this age make decisions in following Christ. These students begin to understand that there are good spirits and bad spirits. The bad spirits are those of satan and the good spirits are those of the Holy Spirit. When students ask Christ to come into their heart as Lord, the Holy Spirit comes in to live within them to help them in making good choices.

The Church Supports the Home

Teachers of 3rd and 4th graders must encourage their children to become involved in a variety of activities to help their child discover their talents and abilities. Encourage them to listen to what their children as to what excites them and if possible, allow their child to experience it. If the student wants to try piano lessons, allow the student to experience taking lessons. If they want to become a boy scout, let them experience being a boy scout. The church must provide activities for children to become involved in and be encouraged to participate. Allow students to try different things, but also remember to never put them above attending Sunday school and church.

We must inform parents how to effectively take what is being taught in the classroom and carry it over for continuation into the home. For example; if students are asked to begin a journal and write in it each day, parents can remind their child to write in it before going to bed each night. Encourage them to read their Bible everyday as well!

As 'paraphrasing' is being discussed in the classroom, ask the parents to include it during family devotion times. Have the parents to allow their children paraphrase Scripture that is being studied or discussed for understanding. As the challenge of family devotions is being presented to the parents, they will learn right along with the children.

These children are readers! The love for reading will either continue or cease at this age. Encourage parents to make it a priority to have their children read daily, especially good Christian material.

Children should never be "pushed" into doing something they are not comfortable with. If they are afraid of heights, they should never be made to jump from something that's high. If they are afraid of the dark, simple let them use a night light. Children should be encouraged to participate, but never pushed. In time, they will face their fears and challenges and step out to take on those things.

While parents are still the greatest influence of this age, parents should be encouraged to talk and listen to their children. This is the time that children should be reminded that they can come and talk to parents about any situation or any feeling they may need to talk about. Children should be reminded that it's normal to want to cry, be angry or experience fear. A relationship between parents and children is critical at this stage because as children get older, they are influenced more and more by their friends. If a personal relationship is not developed now, it will become harder to achieve one as they get older.

Notes to the Teacher

What a fun age to teach! Out of all students, this is probably my favorite age group to teach. They are eager, excited and ready to learn! They can read, write and creatively express themselves. There are many things in their world that they haven't perceived as 'uncool' yet, therefore, they are willing to do just about anything you ask them!

Remember 3 things when teaching these students; Provide new ways for them to learn by teaching in other ways other than just sitting them around the table to listen. Provide opportunities for them to creatively express themselves in what they learn by allowing them to read, write and share their ideas and thoughts; and most of all becoming that 'good listener' that these students really need. Keep close communication going between the class and the home, encouraging the materials being taught in class to be continued at home.

The 8-9 year old student is at a crossroads in their life. At this point, they will enjoy reading and continue doing so for the rest of their lives or realize that reading is boring and something they don't have an interest in doing. These students will also enjoy reading God's Word, viewing it as an exciting Book with stories that really happened to real people like you and I, or think of it as "boring" and "uninteresting". The same with Sunday school...The teacher can make it a fun and exciting place to be or it can be something that children will dread coming to. Those who teach these "middlers" will help them make decisions such as these in how they teach and lead their class.

-9-

"Understanding the Blueprints for Middlers & Teens"

"And, ye fathers, provoke not your children to wrath: but bring them up in the nurture and admonition of the Lord." —Ephesians 6:4

Ministering to 10-12 Year Olds

"Young Adolescence"
"Juniors"

This 5th and 6th grader is undergoing personal transformations physically, emotionally, socially, psychologically, and intellectually. They are leaving childhood and entering into adolescence. Although these 'preteens' think they may not need adult supervision, they still need the love and guidance of an adult who has lots of *"Patience"*.

"Loyal", *"Helpful"* and *"Relational"* best describe this transitioning student as they are leaving their childhood years behind to step into a more 'grown-up' world. They are often referred to as "tweenagers" because they are in between childhood and adolescence. These students are often caught between two worlds…too old for some things and too young for the other things. This can be a real challenge for these students, which causes frustration to the student, as well as their parents.

Physically, "Juniors" increase in their body strength and show continued hand dexterity. Girls are generally as much as two years ahead of boys in physical maturity. Many boys and girls continue their involved in sports, but increasing large muscle movements naturally lead more and more boys into sports. Although some girls continue to be involved in sports, many of them become more interested in other activities that use small muscle movements such as taking piano lessons or sewing.

The 10-12 year old is approaching puberty and may begin to put on some weight and girls may begin to menstruate. Their rapid growth gives them larger appetites, but they have less energy. . Their rapid growth and low energy sometimes dispels them as being "lazy", when in fact, their heart is working extra hard to pump enough blood to their rapidly growing bodies. This causes them to become very tired and experience low energy. Parents must play close attention to their nutritional needs and making sure they get proper rest.

As they are becoming more and more aware of their body, many of them become more fashion conscious. Their "lanky" arms and lengthening legs make them feel as though they look 'awkward', sometimes causing them to appear clumsy. These students, especially girls, are more aware of their personal development and want to wear clothing that is fashionable, yet covering their awkward appearance.

Socially, these preteens are forming stronger, more complex friendships and peer relationships, especially of the same sex. They experience more peer pressure and want to become more and more independent from the family. They seek to be in the "in" crowd and may be pressured to conform to the morals of the group. Parents are still seen as an 'authoritative figure', but they are leaning more towards the opinions and suggestions of their peers. Juniors still need the instruction of parents, but want to make choices on their own. Children who feel good about themselves are more able to resist negative peer pressure and make better choices for themselves. "Juniors" may think they don't need a babysitter or any other adult figure to care for them, when in fact, they really do. Independence should be given in small amounts and increasing as they become more mature, more responsible and older. These students love to be a part of clubs and still love competition (especially those who play sports). They may develop a special interest such as collecting or beginning a new hobby. They enjoy planning and organizing tasks, but often times have difficulty following through.

Emotionally, these preteens begin riding an emotional rollercoaster. The 10-12 year old is great at dramatizing and often develops exaggerated expressions. They may begin to say things such as "nobody loves me" or "you're the worst parents in the world"! Children of this age have may worries and fears and will sometimes appear to be 'emotionally unstable', then the next moment they are wanting hugs and seeking approval. These students will tend to challenge adult knowledge and become more critical of adults. Before, the parent may have been the 'hero', but now they may be seen as the 'villain'. Parent and child relationships are challenged as new emotions are experienced.

This student wants to be involved! They are willing participants who want to help with whatever needs to be done. Teachers will have no problem finding someone to organize the class materials or to assist in giving out Bible. There will be a class full of eager students! As these students are given the ability to make independent choices, it is important that they learn to put God first. As they begin to join community groups or clubs AND keep up with their grades at school, these students will need to learn make good choices and utilize their time so that God, church and Sunday school are not last in their lives.

Theological Concepts of Adolescent Children Ages 10-11

About God

- God is Spirit, who is everywhere, but whose home is in heaven.
- God is all powerful, but He permits evil things to happen.
- God is all wise, but He permits people to choose between Him and sin, even thought He knows what is best.
- God is one, but He is a triune being: Father, Son (Jesus Christ), and Holy Spirit.
- God is absolutely perfect, holy and just.
- God hates all sin.
- God cares for and protects His children.
- God wants to show me His will for my life.

About Jesus	Jesus took on Himself the body of a man so He could do what God had planned. Jesus fulfilled part of God's great plan for me, to bring me to God; I must fulfill the other, to accept what Jesus did on the cross. Jesus shows me how to live for God, for His perfect life is a pattern for all. Jesus took the punishment for the sins of all people on Himself at Calvary. Jesus became alive again and lives in heaven. Jesus Christ was born of a virgin.
About the Bible	The Bible has the answers to all my everyday problems. The Bible can help me live a happy life. The Bible tells the history of God's work among people. The Bible is God's Word, the authority for life. The Bible is set in the culture of another kind of people. I need to understand that culture to understand the Bible. The Bible is without error. The Holy Spirit guided the writers of the Bible books. The Bible is a book to honor and to memorize. It isGod's truth to put into everyday practice. The Bible is God's truth for all people. I need to share it with others. The Bible, which is God's Word, is to be obeyed.
About Home and Parents	My home and parents are part of God's plan for me. My home and parents function as part of God's plan, but I should do my part too. I should show loyalty to my home and parents. I should show honor to my home and parents. I should accept correction from my parents, for this will help me become a strong leader. I should begin to see what makes a Christian home, looking toward the day when I will start one.

About Church and Sunday School	The church is a fellowship of believers in Christ. The church must bring me in contact with church leaders. The church trains me in worship, study, prayer, witness, service and fellowship. The church is a place where I can serve God. The church is a place where I can learn to practice Christian giving and outreach. I can learn about the ordinances.
About Others	Others need my respect for their thoughts, their possessions, their rights. Others need my understanding. Others need my help. I must show others honesty, loyalty, and fair play. Others need my forgiveness. Others need my prayers. Others fit into God's plans, just as I do.
About Angels and Last Things	Satan is the ruler of spiritual wickedness. Satan wants to keep me from coming to God. God has a plan for the future, which will come to pass. People who have trusted Christ as their Savior and have died will be raised from the dead when Christ returns. Satan and his angels will be cast into the lake of fire for eternal punishment. People who have not trusted Christ as their Savior will spend eternity in hell.

What Children Can Learn About the Bible at age 10-12

By now, these students should have a general understanding of basic Bible stories. They may not remember bits and pieces of all of the stories, but should be able to recall some information about each one.

In the Beginning	Adam & Eve	The Garden of Eden
Cain & Abel	Noah & the Flood	The Tower of Babel
Abraham & Sarah	Abraham & Isaac	Hagar & Ishmael

Food for Elijah	10 Lepers	Zacchaeus
Jonah & the Whale	Baby Moses	The Burning Bush
Crossing the Red Sea	10 Commandments	The Golden Calf
The Tabernacle	Cloud & the Fire	Twelve Spies
Wandering in the Wilderness		Samson & Delilah
Hannah	Samuel	David & Goliath
Elijah & the Widow	12 Disciples	Elijah & Prophets of Baal
Elijah Raises Boy from the Dead		Job
Jesus is Born	Jesus As A Boy	Daniel & the Lions Den
The Fiery Furnace	Jonah & the Whale	John the Baptist
Jesus Tempted	Fishers of Men	Friend Through the Roof
Jesus Heals a Cripple	Pool At Bethesda	Jesus Calms A Storm
Jairus Daughter	Feeding of 5,000	Peter Walking on Water
Jesus & the Children	Jesus Heals Blind Man	Lazarus
Good Samaritan	Mary & Martha	Prodigal Son
Blind Bartimaeus	Widow's Mite Judas	Friends: Jonathan & David
Jesus is Crucified	Jesus is Risen	Visiting the Tomb
Doubting Thomas	Disciples Fishing	Jesus Goes Up To Heaven
Peter & John	Paul & Silas	Fruits of the Spirit

Again, this is a repeat of stories that have been taught in the past, but should be taught on a deeper level. Although these students should know many of these stories by now, they should be able to understand them on a much broader and deeper level. For example; instead of just knowing that there were 12 Disciples, they should know something about each one of them and/or maybe able to identify each of them because of something they know about each one individually. Knowing how these students effectively learn and have an understanding of what they know helps us to more effectively teach them in a way that they can understand and make application. We must build a biblical "foundation" so that other deeper truths can be built upon it. They cannot proceed to the next step until they understand first things first.

Remember, helping "Juniors" stay focused on God and make better choices should be our aim in teaching this age group. By already understanding basic concepts about each of these stories, we are able to be more focused in how these students relate personally with each one. If friends are an important part of these students' lives, pull out stories about friends in the Bible and make them relevant in the lives of your students. If making good choices are important, pull out stories of those who made good choices and those who made bad choices so students can see their outcome. When the teacher makes their choices relevant to those choices students make in their lives, it becomes personal to them and students are able to see their own lives within the stories they are studying. Lessons must be relevant, personal and applicable to those we teach.

Connecting to the Bible

Now that we understand some of the characteristics of a child 10-12 years old and know what they can understand, let's make a connection in how they can effectively learn about spiritual things.

Juniors are trying to grow up, but struggle with still being seen as too young. They want to help and become more independent. Workers can use this energy and independence to take on responsibility in the classroom. Students can be given opportunities to take on roles and responsibilities of the class, from putting together lesson booklets, to taking the roll each Sunday morning. More mature students may be assigned a part of the lesson to teach the rest of the class! Choose an artistic individual who is good with arts and crafts to lead everyone in an art project that is planned for the lesson. Giving these students opportunity within the classroom will teach them responsibility and will provide them a chance to serve.

As you plan activities for these students, administer caution when planning events such as lock-ins or activities with extended physical exertion. Remember, their bodies are growing at such a rapid pace, their heart if fighting to pump enough blood to accommodate it, thus causing them to tire more easily. As you schedule all night events and physical activities, allow them periods of rest or sleep.

We learned that these '*tweenagers*' want to be accepted by their peers, therefore their morals may be challenged. The teacher can prepare lessons, incorporating issues such as making choices and the repercussions of those choices. Lessons from the Bible such as "Peter Walks On the Water", "Samson & Delilah" and "4 Men in the Fiery Furnace" that teach students about making good choices and staying focused on God. We also learned that these students are emotionally challenged. Lessons concerning attitudes and how to handle emotions must be taught to help juniors deal with them. The story of Job allows the students to see an individual deal with so many emotions, yet stayed focused on God. Anger, bitterness, jealousy and confusion are all emotions these juniors deal with, while teachers must reinforce to students how God gave us emotions, but we must learn to keep them under control. The "Fruits of the Spirit" makes a great lesson as students learn ways to better handle and control their emotions. Workers should also remind students that it is good to have someone to talk to and 'vent' their feelings. Encourage them to talk to their parents or a good Christian friend for advice and support. Teachers should always let their students know that they are available if they need someone to talk to.

Parent relationships can become critical at this age; therefore a good parent-child relationship should be encouraged. As you plan lessons and activities for your class, plan some events that will include parents. Doing a character study? Allow both parent and student to do the research together in class over a three week period. Are you saying the parent comes to the Sunday school class with their child for three week? Yes! Not only does this give them an opportunity to learn about the Bible together, but it allows the parent to grasp an idea about what is actually takes place inside the classroom. Activities outside the class could be "Take your mom to lunch" week or how about an "overnight camp out" with father and son? Plan any activities that would encourage positive parent-child relationships. What about those in the class who do not have a mother or father unavailable? Encourage them to invite someone who is like a mother or father figure to them. This will also encourage them to develop other adult relationships and give them someone else to talk to other than a parent. Remember, some children may not feel comfortable telling some things to their parents.

Teachers must stress the need to follow rules and obey authority figures. This includes being respectful and being appreciative towards those inside and outside the church. Pastors, church leaders, parents, policemen, government, school teachers, principals, etc...

The Church Supports the Home

Parents must learn and understand this stage of development in their child at this age. Many parents will make comments such as "I don't know what is going on with my daughter, but she has become a monster at home!" Schedule a short meeting with them to discuss this developmental stage and what they can expect (unless they are already experiencing it). As a teacher, let them know that you will be working with on ways to encourage the parent-child relationship, while teaching them spiritually how to handle many of the challenges they will face at this stage. Parents need to know that their child is 'normal' and that many children have a tougher time going through this adolescent stage than others. Workers can give parents an idea of what they hope to accomplish in the classroom so that it can be reinforced at home. Taking responsibilities, reinforcing rules, being respectful and maintaining discipline should be among those things.

At this point, there is a greater emphasis on the role of the father in the home. Young adolescents need direction in their lives and the guidance of an individual who has a loyalty to Christ; someone the student admires and a godly example of a servant. What better person should that be than the father? We realize that the church is not made up of whole families, but many of them are made up of blended families. Many fathers have become 'absent' from the home, not only because they don't live there, but because they are working or have other commitments that have pulled them away from the home. Encourage the fathers of these students to take their role as being head of the household (Ephesians 5:22-27) in leading the home and reinforcing the work of the church by continuing its teaching in the home.

Encourage the parents to give household responsibilities to the student. These tasks should be done correctly and completely. If giving allowances, begin discussing saving and spending money wisely. Goal setting is necessary and rules should be followed. Parents should know their children's friends and their families. Hero worship is still prevalent for this student (see Ages 8-9).

Notes to the Teacher

The teacher can be the connection between the home and the church. It will be important for the teacher to communicate on an on-going basis with the parents of those they teach. Many of these young adolescence will begin to experience many emotions and encounter frustration and confusion. Teachers must be firm in their rules and expectations, while lovingly guiding the student. They must be 'watching' and 'listening' for different behaviors and gently help direct them and their parents through them. Talents and abilities have surfaced by now, therefore we should help students to identify their own personal abilities and encourage them to develop them. For example; if we see artistic abilities in the student, we should encourage the parent to seek avenues to develop that talent or provide opportunities to share their gift. Someone in the class may be a creative writer and should be challenged to develop that talent by taking additional classes at school or by providing ways for them to share their creative writing with others. When we help students focus on what they are good at, we are helping them build their self-esteem by cultivating gifts that could possibly be used in kingdom building. Teachers should seek ways for students to use their individual talents and abilities within the church.

Ministering to Students 13-15

"Early Adolescence"

Students of this age are considered to be in early "Adolescence". These 7th, 8th and 9th grade students are leaving behind a "child's world" and entering into a more mature, adult-like environment. Some words to describe this student could be *"identity seekers"* and *"Testers"*. These students are moving towards independence.

Children in early adolescence will experience rapid physical changes throughout the body. These children not only transform physically, but grow emotionally and begin thinking in more mature ways. Physically, the child will enter puberty. The girls will mature quicker than the boys and often adapt to group activities of the same sex. These students are so worried about being "normal" that they will often see themselves as less than others, especially if they see their peers developing quicker than they are. Girls will tend to become overly sensitive about their weight because of the rapid weight gain associated with puberty. A small percentage of adolescent girls (1-3%) become so obsessed with their weight that they develop severe eating disorders such as anorexia nervosa or bulimia.

The early adolescent becomes very self-conscious in adapting to a transforming body, but also struggles with their identity. Their emerging identity is shaped over time by internal and external influences. These teens integrate the opinions and influences of others with their own likes and dislikes. The goal is to develop secure identities where they know where they fit and don't want to fit. A healthy self-esteem is very important to these students because it influences the kinds of friends they will seek and the choices they will make.

As they are growing rapidly, they may appear clumsy as they try to adjust with this "awkward" growth spurt. As their bodies are rapidly growing, their bodies need to adjust and repair. This age needs about 9 ½ hours of sleep each night.

Friends and peers become more influential to them as these students begin to "pull away" from parents, but some will occasionally tend to return to childish behavior. Their close friendships gain importance, while less attention is shown to parents. Friendships influence them in their interests and clothing styles. Though often moody, they are more likely to express feelings by actions rather than by words. The early adolescent is mostly interested in the present and the near future.

These teens are *"testers"*. They will tend to push rules to their limit to see how far they can go. If these teens can get by with a little, they will continue to get by with more and more until there are no rules. Teens want structure and want to know that parents expect the rules to be followed. When they are in their rooms, they may want to keep the door shut or request more privacy. These teens will often become more argumentative and question adults' values and judgments. They shy away from being seen with their parents in public and may begin to interact with parents as people by asking more questions.

Theological Concepts of Students Ages 13-15

Theological concepts of students ages 13-15 should be that of an adult, with an emphasis on more "how to's". By this time, these students should have a good foundation of basic Bible knowledge and are ready to go a little "deeper" with Bible study. The depth I am speaking of includes not only knowing about basic stories, but having the knowledge of doing effective study and to be able to look up facts and meanings.

Earlier, we discussed the need to do character studies or customs in which students will feel a "part of" and to identify with what is being taught. Now, it is important that these students understand different books of the Bible and major events that took place within each one. Students will be more apt to identify with stories and events found in the New Testament than those of the Old Testament. When students can grasp a general knowledge of Books of the Bible and some of the major events covered in each one, it will help direct them to easily discover more information for effective study. For example, if a student wants to learn more about the end times, they would know that they should look at the Book of Revelation. Here are some other examples these students should know:

Genesis - Creation
Exodus - Moses, Ten Commandments, burning bush, building the tabernacle
Job - Maintaining your faith through trials
Galatians - Fruits of the Spirit
Psalms - Book of Praise
Proverbs - Book of Wisdom
Daniel - Three Hebrew Children, Daniel & the Lions Den
Matthew, Mark, Luke, John - (4 Gospels and The life of Christ)
Acts - the early church
Romans - the "Roman Road" (Plan of Salvation)
Hebrews - Faith
James - Basic Christian Living

These are just some of the examples of the books of the Bible and its overall thesis. As these students study and certain events come to their minds, they are able to locate Scripture more quickly and be familiar with events in and around what they are studying.

Another great thing for students to learn at this age is different study aides and how to use them. The Bible is full of symbolisms, customs and cultures that are not identified in Scripture. Discovering meaning and purpose underlying events and stories of the Bible gives the student a greater understanding behind what is taking place in the story and could give explanation in its understanding.

Here are some study aides that this age group can learn to use for effective Bible study:

Bible Dictionary - This dictionary is a book that includes definitions and explanatory articles on every Bible subject. Some dictionaries include maps, charts, illustrations and drawings for more in-depth study.

Concordance - A concordance is a book that gives listings of words and Scripture references where they can be found. A person may think of a Scripture and not know where it is in the Bible. The person can think of a key word in a Scripture, look it up in the concordance and determine where it is found in the Bible. Many Bibles include a concordance, but these concordances are limited.

Expository Dictionary - An expository dictionary is a book that gives definitions of Hebrew and Greek words found in the Old and New Testament.

Commentary - A commentary is a book that gives more in-depth explanation based on personal opinion. Many commentaries are written giving verse by verse explanation as well as entire chapters or Books of the Bible.

There are also different types of Bible and versions of the Bible that can be looked at and discussed:

Life Application Bible
NIV Study Bible
Student Bible
King James Version Bible
New Living Translation Bible
Parallel Bible

Introducing study aides will broaden their skills and help students gain a greater knowledge of the Bible and help them to understand its meaning.

The Church Supports the Home

The greatest task the church can perform is to support the homes is to encourage parents to continue bringing their children to church and being spiritual leaders for them. Many parents of this age group have a difficult time emotionally with these young teens. Their mood swings, argumentative spirits and influences can cause the atmosphere of the home to become quite "explosive", bringing about poor relationships within the family. Communicating to the parents about what these students are going through and assuring them that this is a "normal" phase for many of this age will be a source of encouragement to them.

Encourage parents to set rules and then stand on what they say. Although we realize that these kids will push their limits, they need to understand what is expected and where their boundaries are. The same works for discipline. Parents should be in agreement on rules and punishments for their children. Children should know what the rules are and the consequences for breaking them. Parents should follow through and expect their children to adhere to them. These teens should understand that they are given parents to guide and instruct them while here on this earth, therefore we should be obedient (Ephesians 6:1,2). When we are disobedient to our parents, we are being disobedient to God!

The church can minister to the parents of this group by providing parenting classes. These classes could cover issues that parents struggle with such as discipline, setting rules and establishing boundaries. Other issues could include giving responsibilities, completing tasks, handling money and time management. Two great things come out of parenting classes; parents receive helpful information and advice on dealing with issues with their teen; and they come in contact with other parents who struggle with some of the same issues. Through these classes, a network of parental support could be found and new relationships could be formed from them.

Parents should remind students to spend some time reading Christian material, reading their Bible and praying. Teens enjoy journaling and should be encouraged to keep one. Parents should be aware of what music their teen is listening to, what movies they are viewing and what friends they are hanging around with. A good youth program at the church will provide a network of friends for students to do many of these activities with, while being influenced by them. Teachers and youth leaders must build a trust with their students by developing relationships with them. Many of these students will come and share their hearts with leaders before talking to their parents. Often times, these leaders are "bridges" of communication between parent and student.

Note to the Teacher

Don't be discouraged if you get lots of moans and groans when it comes to your students doing work! They connect this kind of 'schooling' with what they get in the secular school and already have a perception that it will be boring. Remember, your students will only be as excited as you are! Approach your class with excitement and with an attitude of anticipation. How the project is presented to the class will determine whether the students want to be a part of it.

As students do the research, provide ways for them to share what they have learned with others. Make plans for them to share it with students in another class or even present this material to the entire church! A great idea is to gather all their information and put it in booklet form for every student to have. Allow the students to gather the information, write or type the material and put it together as a class. Make these booklets available to others within your church.

Communication between the youth worker and the parent is important. Keep parents informed on the progress of their child in the classroom. Many times, parents are only hearing the negative things from their school or from other people. It is refreshing to hear something good that their child has done or is participating in. Sometimes your positive remarks are what help get them through the week. Do not only give these positive remarks to the parents, but make sure you communicate these remarks to your students. They need to know your feelings towards their performance in the classroom. Noticing something special about a student and their ability to do well will speak multitudes to them and encourage them to continue the work. Life gets us so busy sometimes, we don't stop and we overlook the things that need to be noticed the most.

-10-

"Understanding the Blueprints for Young Adults"

"Remember now thy Creator in the days of thy youth..." —Ecclesiastes 12:1

Ministering to Students Ages 15-17

"Middle Adolescence"

Students, ages 15-17 are considered to be a replica of those ages 13-15, except more stabilized. These teens are still dealing with fluctuating emotions and are greatly influenced by their peers. Self-image is still very important to them and if affected by their personal successes in sports, school and how well they are meeting the expectations of their parents. They worry about failure and continue to push towards independence. Words to describe these teens could be or *"Experiencers" or "Examiners"*.

Physically, these high school students have entered puberty and will complete their physical transition from childhood to adult. Females will nearly reach their adult height, while males continue to grow into their early twenties. Emotionally, they may go through periods of sadness, which may spark more of an interest in writing their feelings. Their ability to handle the rigors of a more demanding schedule improves because of the memory and organizational abilities. They take greater pride in their work and are able to set goals. These teens are so influenced by their friends, they have a greater tendency to try new things. Often they may try many of the wrong things such as drugs and alcohol. Students of this age are attracted to the opposite sex with feelings of love and passion.

Because of their newfound abilities, the 15-17 year old may think "he knows it all" and can be very difficult to deal with. They still do not have the life skills needed to be self-sufficient; therefore it is important that parents and leaders continue to guide them in making good choices. *"Experiencers"* are learning to drive, taking on part-time jobs and gaining new opportunities for independence. They must be reminded and informed about the dangers of making bad choices, specifically on sex, alcohol and the influence of others. One bad decision could change the rest of their lives. As *"Examiners"*, these teens are not only looking at themselves physically as being attractive to the opposite sex, they are examining themselves to consider future plans. Most students of this age are asked to choose a career path in high school in which they will take classes to accomplish their career interests. Strong role models and mentors should encourage students to pursue their talents and abilities and assist in pointing them in the right direction.

Theological Concepts of Ages 15-17

The theological concepts of students ages 15-17 are that of an adult with the emphasis on "opportunity" and "Guidance". Previously, we discovered that by the time the student becomes a teen, they should be familiar with basic Bible knowledge. Once they have gained this knowledge, they should be encouraged to learn how to develop study skills for effective Bible study and to deepen the knowledge they have learned. We discussed teaching them how to use different study aides to help develop meaningful study. Now that students have the head knowledge, let's give them the opportunity to use it. By now, their talents and abilities have surfaced. If the teacher has spent any time with them at all, they will have learned the student's strengths and weaknesses.

When their strengths have been identified, the church must encourage students to use them for God. If a student has an ability to sing, encourage them to use their voice to sing at one of the church services. If a teen displays gifts of evangelism, point them in the direction of visitation or missions. If a student has a gift of working with young children, get them in touch with your children's ministry to possibly help with a class or camp! Their talents and abilities, along with God's leading, may inspire them to give their lives to fulltime Christian Service.

Titus 2 gives us instructions to teach our younger people not only in word, but by example. How are they going to ever know about reaching out to others if we never give them a chance to act upon it. It is not enough to simply know God's Word, but we must put it in practice!

As students are studying events and stories of the Bible, seek ways for them to demonstrate what they have learned. For example, if you are teaching a lesson in which your students are inspired to "...love your neighbor as yourself" (Mark 12:33), seek ways in which the class can demonstrate that love. Visiting an elderly neighbor who has no family, helping a single mom mow the yard or taking dinner to a sick church member are all good examples of "loving your neighbor".

This age group also needs to learn how to accept responsibility. Allowing them to perform a task, even if they fail, will give them an idea of what the adult world is all about. One way the church can accomplish this is to have a "Youth Week". Church staff members can adopt a teen and teach them their job. That student performs that job (under the supervision of the adult) throughout that week. On Sunday, allow that student to step in to that position for that day. For example, a student may have a love for music. They are paired up with the music director and the teen is taught the basic fundamentals of the position. On Sunday, that individual may direct the congregation in worship music or lead the choir in a song. An event such as this allows students to not only step in and do ministry, but also teaches them about the time and commitment that really goes in to that position. Other positions to fill during "Youth Week" could be deacon, secretary, usher, Sunday school teacher, youth Pastor and even Pastor.

When students become seniors in high school, it is a good idea to begin transitioning them into the "College & Career Class" at church. As seniors, they are no longer caught up in the 'pep rallies' or the 'crush' they have on that person in their history class, but are more interested in future events and activities. A student's senior year is a great time to prepare them for what is going to take place in their lives in the months ahead. This transition will help students adjust and adapt to some major things, so they won't be so overwhelmed.

The Church Supports the Home

The church can help the homes of these high school students by providing opportunities for serving, education and fellowship. These students are making plans and decisions about what to do with the rest of their lives and need guidance in helping find them. We must remember that when it comes to Christian service, we are providing "on the job training". The church must strategically seek ways to teach and train these young students to serve in the church. These students make excellent assistant teachers, nursery workers and music assistants!

Earlier, we discussed the need for youth workers to build relationships with their students. No doubt, these students will come to you seeking advice on what to do. By asking your advice on such an important issue should confirm that they trust your judgment and will consider what you have to share with them. Teachers need to take note of special talents and abilities of the students and help guide them in that direction. Teachers should get to know the local high school counseling staff to gain knowledge about various colleges and careers to possibly suggest to the student. Many will go to college, while others will choose a technical path or simple step into a job following high school. While we should always encourage education, we must realize that college is not for everyone. Encourage students to look into a vocational school to learn a trade or a skill that will give them the training to get a good job.

Let's not overlook students who have the desire to give their lives to fulltime Christian service. Our youth are our future church leaders and should be encouraged to take this path, if desired. As youth leaders see this potential and desire in their students, they should talk to the church pastor. The church pastor may sit down with that student and pray with them about their heart for Christian service. The church can recommend Bible colleges and seminaries that will give them the education and training desired.

Some students will not attend college due to financial reasons. The church can help by establishing a scholarship to award to a student to help with college classes and tuition expenses. A one year scholarship to the local community college could be the start the student needs to get them going in the right direction.

The church can host an "education night" in which individuals in a variety of fields can come and share what they do and the education needed to work in that area. By doing so, students can gain information about that field, while being able to ask questions to someone who works in that area.

The church can host a special "graduation" service, honoring them upon graduation from high school. Set aside a time at a morning service that students can wear their caps and gowns, walk down the aisle of the church and be recognized for their accomplishments. The pastor may issue a challenge to these students as they pursue their dreams and encourage them to continue their walk with God. As each student is recognized, the pastor may share the student's educational goals, while presenting them a certificate or a small gift from the church. The pastor should offer a prayer for the student, while challenging the congregation to continue to pray for them as they step out on this new journey.

If your church should decide to host this graduation recognition service, plan ahead and make it special for the students and their families. Planning ahead will allow students to invite their friends and family to this service (there may be some attending looking for a church!). Serve cake and punch following the service and have a photographer to take pictures of the graduates and their families. You may want to go a step further and present the graduate with a framed picture of themselves with a verse from the Bible. A good verse could be one from Jeremiah 29:11 *"For I know the plans I have for you", declares the Lord, "the plans to prosper you and not to harm you, plans to give you hope and a future."* Purposeful and meaningful events such as this will be remembered for a lifetime.

Notes to the Teacher

To the student, the teacher could become a lifelong friend. As the teacher or youth worker sets them out on this new journey, they can continue to be an influential person in their lives. As the student graduates college, marries their lifetime mate and begins a family of their own, the high school teacher can continue a friendship that will follow them for the rest of their lives. If possible, help them celebrate some of their "milestones" that occur, along with being prayerfully supportive during the difficult times. Attending their graduation, visiting their home following the birth of their child or attending the funeral of a lost family member will speak to their hearts and demonstrate your love and care for them. Many times, if students are asked what they remembered most about growing up in the church, the greatest response will be "my Sunday school teacher".

If there is one thought that could be driven into the hearts and minds of these high school students, it would be to ALWAYS seek God first, then add the other stuff. Students are so busy with school activities, working, making plans for college, etc…many of them will not make God and church attendance a priority. This is the first step for many of them to gradually fall out of church. According to George Barna, 70% of all high school graduates that leave and go away to college, never come back to the church.

A story was told about a teacher who was teaching her class one day and had an illustration to show. She took a quart jar and proceeded to fill it with big rocks about the size of pin pong balls or a little larger. After she filled the jar up with the rocks, she asked the class, "do you think the jar is full'? The class responded, "Yes". The teacher told the class that the jar was not full and proceeded to add smaller rocks to the same jar, filling it up to the top. She asked the class again, "Do you think the jar is full"? Again, the class responded, "Yes". The teacher corrected the class and began to add sand, filling up all of the little crooks and craneys. She asked the class, "Now, do you think the jar is full now"? The class responded with a "Yes". The teacher told the class that it was NOT full and proceeded to pour water into the jar. After the water had reached the top of the jar, she asked the class one last time, "Do you think this jar is full"? This illustration teaches us about more than only filling your life (the jar) with a lot of things (rocks, sand, water,) and there's always room for more, but teaches us a lesson that if we don't add the big things first, the other stuff won't fit. Matthew 6:33 says *"But seek ye first the kingdom of God, and his righteousness; and all these things shall be added unto you."* No matter how much we have to do in our lives, we must always seek God and His ways first, and then He will make a way for us to do the other things. For these students, it will be continuing to come to church and cultivating a hot heart through prayer and the study of God's Word. Parents are still the rule setters and care givers at this age, therefore they must be encouraged to continue to bring their teens to church and to faithfully remain active in its services and activities.

Ministering to Adults Ages 18-24

"Late Adolescence"
"The Lost Generation"

Young adolescence ages 18-24 are entering into a different, yet new, chapter in their lives. These individuals are establishing goals and setting the foundation for the rest of their lives. Now, they have stepped into the world of adulthood, leaving their childhood behind. Some words to describe these individuals are *"Seekers*" and *"Independent"*.

The late adolescent has a firmer identity of themselves, while moving towards greater independence. They are able to think through ideas and concepts, while becoming more concerned for the future. Physically, they have reached their growth potential, while boys may continue growing in height into their early twenties. Emotionally, they have reached greater stability and have become self reliant and are able to make independent decisions.

The future is of great interest to them because they are *"seeking"* as to what to do with the rest of their lives. While many of them will move away from home and go to college, there will be some who will continue to live close to home and attend the local university. Some of these students may opt to work a while before making decisions about their educational careers, while others will make the decision to not pursue college at all. Students of this age may change career goals several times before making a final decision. This tends to happen because these students may be exposed to other areas of greater interest or they may find themselves pursuing something that really doesn't interest them at all. Although many students will move away to go to college, some of them will return home to pick up where they left off.

Most of these students are working full time jobs, going to school and are adapting to *independence*. They are learning to handle money, responsibility, schedules and priorities. For many of them, they are paying bills, washing their own clothes, and cooking their own meals. This will be a lot of responsibility as they will learn to adjust in doing many of these things in their own way and in their own time. The key to their success in gaining independence is to make sure they have the "know how" so that they can put this knowledge into practice. With this new gained "independence", these students are at a greater risk for making mistakes. By now, these students should be aware of the price for making poor choices. Experience is sometimes the best teacher, so these students should have the opportunity to make some mistakes and learn from the mistakes they make.

Good role models are a must for this young adolescent. Successful adults who have good educations, good jobs, great marriages and exciting lives will be an influence to them. Friends and family should encourage these students to surround themselves with good role models.

Life will not be laid out and the same roads will not always be taken. Some of these young adults may get married or even begin a family before graduating college. This group can be a mix of people at different places in their lives. Statistics are showing that many of these young people are waiting until their upper twenties before getting married and starting families.

Theological Concepts of Late Adolescence Ages 18-24

Students of this age should have knowledge of the Bible basics and know how to effectively study the Bible on their own. While this should be continued, we must now take another step in reaching and teaching these students. Throughout this book, we've discussed the importance of "life application" and how necessary it is to provide ways for students to see themselves within the pages of Scripture. Now, we have entered a time where teachers and leaders can take necessary skills that students of this age need and address them from the perspective of God's Word. Here are some topics that these students need and are of interest to them. These classes should also be included in their Christian Education:

Goal Setting	Budgeting/Finances	Time Management
Stress Management	Marriage/Parenting	Spiritual Gifts
Relationships	Overcoming Obstacles	And others!

Students of this age are experiencing the *"real world"* and we need to help them deal with issues they will face. Christ is not only interested in us spiritually, but He cares about our jobs, homes, families and our finances! When we are outside of the church and in to the world, this is where we put our Christian education in motion. People that we work with, go to school with or have relationships with may never set foot in our churches, therefore, we must allow them to see God working in and through us. God's Word tells us how to be good stewards of our money. God's Word gives instructions on how to be a good spouse and parent. When we strive to do our best with what God blesses us with, He will be faithful to do His part.

These young adults are learning life skills that will affect the rest of their lives. What they do with their money now will set the stage for their financial future. The goals they set educationally and personally will have affective on other phases of their lives. Learning how to deal with stress and better time management will help them to accomplish what God has for them. God want them to be the best they can be and to manage what He gives them to the best of their ability.

These students are often referred to as "the lost generation". They are given this name because many churches provide very little in teaching this age. Either they are teens, or they are adults. These young students are transitioning into becoming adults; therefore the church is recognizing the need for curriculum to minister to this "in between generation". Writers are now beginning to produce age appropriate curriculum to spiritually meet the needs of this age. Because of the high statistics of these students dropping out of church, we must minister to them while we have them by providing materials that will teach and train through topics that are relevant to them and that interest them.

The Church Supports the Home

It should be the desire of the church to build and grow strong, spiritually healthy homes. When the home is strong, the church is strong because the church is made up of homes. At this stage, these young students are beginning to lay foundations for the new home they will create and build in the near future. What we teach them now will assist in determining the kind of home they will have. What we do with this age group is directly affecting their "personal" home.

The best way for the church to assist these "new" future home builders is to continue to provide ways to teach and train them in the areas relevant to them. The church can also provide opportunities for this group to fellowship and build a network of friends with other young adults their age. This can be done by allowing these students to offer opportunities to bring other young adults into the church or to provide a way for the church to step out and minister outside their four walls, such as with a student campus ministry at the local college. Guest speakers, mission trip opportunities, concerts and classes are just a few of the ways the church can minister to these students. With guidance, these students should be allowed to plan and implement these activities, giving them responsibilities and allowing them to serve.

Notes to the Teacher

Leaders of this area must remember that all students may not be in the same place in their lives. The class must provide ministry to those who are single as well as those who are married. The teacher will not only serve as teacher of the Bible to these students, but will serve as mentor and as an example. These students need guidance, counsel and instruction.

It will be very important for the teacher to provide opportunities for fellowship. Short trips and activities are enjoyed by all, including the teacher. While these students are old enough to be responsible for themselves, the teacher does not have to be afraid of leaving them alone without adult supervision. Going out of town for seminars on topics that interest them, camping, canoeing, hiking, etc…are all great ways for students to have a good time, while building friendships within their group. Usually finances are of great importance, so 'free' entertainment and gatherings appeal to them.

These students like to "hang out" by having Bible studies in their homes. Because of their newfound "independent" living, students will be eager to invite the group to their 'cribs' for Bible study and fellowship. Students can host cookouts and movie nights for minimal or no cost.

Part Four

The Inspection

-11-

"Blueprints for Evaluating the Structure"

"According to the grace of God which is given unto me, as a wise masterbuilder, I have laid the foundation, and another buildeth thereon. But let every man take heed how he buildeth thereupon." —I Corinthians 3:10

Completing the Project

Now that the classes are lined up and the teachers in place and the curriculum has been ordered, what is needed is a vehicle to keep the momentum going and to insure success in your endeavors to have a successful and meaningful Sunday School program.

Inspections

Periodically, there should be inspections of the program much as one would encounter in building a house. These inspections or evaluations are not done to find fault with anyone or anything, but to ensure that the program is progressing in the manner in which it was designed. These evaluations may be done by the Superintendent of Sunday school or by the Christians Education director of the church. Each worker and teacher should be aware of the process and be informed as to how they may assist in the process. Investigation should be made as to ascertain whether or not the objectives and goals of the Sunday school are being met, if the educational program is following its purpose statement and if lives are actually being changed by the Christian education ministry. Questions should be formulated in such a fashion that their answers would reveal the true status of the Sunday school program. Many things are easy to evaluate, especially when they involve numbers. It is very easy to see if your attendance has increased. However, it may be more difficult to determine if actual Bible knowledge is being assimilated by the students. The authors of this book strongly recommend periodic testing of the students to see if the teaching techniques and methods used actually produce results; if not a closer look at the teaching methods being employed needs to be done. In addition a survey of the students to determine if they find the teaching techniques beneficial and motivating should also be conducted. For too many years the teaching of the Bible has been seen as nothing more than a Sunday morning activity with no real goals and nothing to show whether or not we have been successful. Having periodic times of evaluation will demonstrate that we are serious about Christian Education in the church.

Evaluations

After completing the testing, surveys, and observations, the Christian education staff needs to evaluate the findings. After evaluating the findings plans should be made to make improvements where needed. It may be discovered that some classes need to be moved or split. Much care needs to be exercised here in order not to discourage or dishearten those who attend the classes. The educator needs to be aware of close friendships that may have developed among the members of a class and take care not to do anything that would disrupt the fellowship. If a class needs to be split it could be done along lines of gender. Some questions that need to be answered are: "Have the overall goals of the Sunday School been met? Can we see real change in the lives of the students? Have our attendance goals been met? Is the curriculum adequate for each age group? Is there a good teacher-student ratio? Do all teachers have an assistant? Are the classrooms adequate in size? How do we go about affecting change? Are there teachers or workers that need to be replaced? If so, how will we do that?

Another area that needs to be considered is the area of teacher training. The Christian education staff needs to plan on having the necessary training to equip each teacher to do the best job they can. At least one seminar or workshop should be conducted each year. Areas of concern should be encouragement, resources, and curriculum and teaching methods. Many times teachers and workers are recruited, given an assignment and never interacted with unless they miss Sunday school or someone reports them teaching things that are contrary to the churches' beliefs and practices. Every educational team needs to develop plans and methods whereby they will consistently and periodically give encouragement to teachers and workers along with expressing gratitude for their service. In addition each teacher and workers needs to be made aware that any resource need will be met by the church. Every effort should be made not to tie the hands of those who have the responsibility of teaching our children in the ways of God. After conducting the seminars, workshops, etc. each teacher should be asked if the training session met their needs. This author has attended workshops that were nothing more than an advertisement for materials and curriculum and had very little to offer in the way of teacher training. It is a waste of time to ask a teacher or worker to attend a training session and not give them anything that will help in their work. Remember our goal is to be effective in our teaching and to constantly evaluate and adjust our methods to make sure this happens.

Here are some evaluation examples that could prove helpful in evaluating your Sunday school program:

Personal Evaluation of the Sunday School

We need your help in improving our Sunday school!

Please fill out the following questionnaire and share your personal views about the following items based on your own experience teaching Sunday school:

How Are We Doing?

	Excellent	Good	Fair	Poor
Outreach	4	3	2	1
Evangelism	4	3	2	1
Ministry	4	3	2	1
Fellowship	4	3	2	1
Material Content	4	3	2	1
Overall Sunday school	4	3	2	1

We're doing a good job of ___________________________________

____.

We need to work on ____

____.

Please share your suggestions and improvements: ________________

____

____.

Progress We Have Made

Compared to last year, we have achieved the following:

	Improved	Stayed the Same	Declined
Outreach	3	2	1
Evangelism	3	2	1
Ministry	3	2	1
Fellowship	3	2	1
Material Content	3	2	1
Overall Sunday School	3	2	1

I feel like we have made the most progress in ______________________.

I wish we would ____

____

____.

Year End Evaluation

This evaluation will allow the leadership to establish specific area goals and to better identify goals which have and have not been met.

1. Enrollment Goal: ____.

Last Year: ________ Current Year: ________

Was goal achieved? ____________

Evaluation: ____

____.

2. Visitors/Prospects Goal: ________________________________.

Last Year: ________ Current Year: ________

Was goal achieved? ____________

Evaluation: ____

____.

3. Units/Classes Goal: ____________________________________.

Last Year: ________ Current Year: ________

Was goal achieved? ____________

Evaluation: ____

____.

4. Class Size Goals/Student Ratio: ______________________________.

Last Year: _________ Current Year: _________

Was goal achieved? ______________

Evaluation: ____

____.

5. Workers Goal: (*Ex: 2 per class*) ______________________________.

Last Year: _________ Current Year: _________

Was goal achieved? ______________

Evaluation: ____

____.

6. Workers In Training Goal: (Ex: each worker attend training monthly & 2 outside training conferences within a year) __________________________.

Last Year: ________ Current Year: __________

Was goal achieved? ______________

Evaluation: ____

____.

7. Sunday School Leadership Training Goal: *(Ex: Directors/Leaders meet to plan)* ____.

Last Year: ________ Current Year: ___________

Was goal achieved? ______________

Evaluation: ____

____.

8. Sunday school Attendance Goal: ____________________________.

Last Year: __________ Current Year: ___________

Average Attendance: ______________

Enrollment: ______________________

Percentage: ______________________

Evaluation: ____

____.

9. Saved/Baptisms Goals from Sunday school: ______________________.

Last Year:__________ Current Year: ___________

Saved:_________________

Baptized: ______________

Overall Percentage: ____________

Evaluation: ____

____.

10. Number of New Teacher Goals: ____________________________.

Last Year: _________ Current Year: __________

Evaluation: ____

____.

Worker's Training Evaluation

We need your help in evaluating our training sessions. Please take a moment to answer the following questions as honest as possible.

1. Do you plan one on one meetings with your assistant?
   Yes_______ No________

2. Do you attend the scheduled training sessions provided by the church?
   Usually_______ Sometimes_________ Never________

3. Following are several statements about our training sessions. Please indicate how you personally feel about each statement:

Statement	Agree	Maybe	Disagree	N/O
My time in training is well spent.	_____	_____	_____	_____
The resources for training are adequate	_____	_____	_____	_____
The scheduled time for training is good	_____	_____	_____	_____
I find the training sessions are very informative.	_____	_____	_____	_____

4. How do you think the training sessions help you in teaching your class? Please rate the following:

Statement	Agree	Maybe	Disagree	N/O
Communication is shared between workers	_____	_____	_____	_____
The sessions give me creative teaching ideas.	_____	_____	_____	_____
Sessions motivate me to be a team player.	_____	_____	_____	_____
Sessions help with problem solving.	_____	_____	_____	_____
Sessions inspire me to better teach.	_____	_____	_____	_____

5. Following are 5 purposes we strive to accomplish during the sessions. Please evaluate how well we are accomplishing each purpose.

Statement	Excellent	Good	Fair	Poor
PROMOTION	_____	_____	_____	_____
PREPARATION	_____	_____	_____	_____
PLANNING	_____	_____	_____	_____
PROBLEM SOLVING	_____	_____	_____	_____
PERSONAL SUPPORT	_____	_____	_____	_____

Comments and Suggestions: ______________________________

____.

How to Conduct a Meeting

Scheduling and conducting meetings are an integral part of any organization and the Christian educational program of the church is no different. It is necessary to have meetings where we make plans, evaluate our plans and readjust our plans. But how should these meetings be conducted? Are there principles, methods or strategies that will ensure that our meetings are productive and supportive of our educational staff and program? This article will attempt to identify those things that can be employed to make meetings enjoyable and productive.

In scheduling meetings it must be remembered that planning ahead is important. Last minute meetings only serve to bring frustration as those whom we are targeting often are not able to attend due to the fact they have not had ample opportunity to make plans for the meeting. Meetings should be scheduled well enough in advance to give everyone ample opportunity to make plans to attend. In addition only conduct meetings that are necessary. If you only need to give out information with little or no interaction then emails or memos will do the job.

Seating is important. If you plan on using white boards, projections screens, etc. make sure each person has an unobstructed view. If there are special guests make sure appropriate seating is provided and each guest is properly recognized.

Honor the time of everyone involved. Set a beginning and end time for the meeting and stick to it. Staying within the allotted time is a good way to keep people on track and make the most of the time. It will also give you an opportunity to tactfully interrupt statements that are counterproductive or of no value by saying, "We only have so much time, so let's stay on the subject." Starting on time demonstrates that you respect the time, opinions, and feelings of all attending. If you wait until Jim arrives you are by inference saying the meeting doesn't start at ten; it starts when Jim arrives. This in effect, saying that Jim is more important than all the others. Surely you want to reward those who come on time and not those who arrive late.

At the beginning of the meeting let everyone know the purpose of the meeting and what you hope to expect during your time together. Set ground rules. If the participants are expected to contribute to the conversation, let them know. If they are expected to keep their remarks within a specified length of time, make sure they are aware of it. Give participants an opportunity to contribute and if they are not offer them the floor. However, make sure you are not putting them on the spot. Hold people to the things they have said or committed to earlier in the meeting or in previous meetings. Point out contradictions in what people say and encourage the group to resolve these contradictions. Examine body language for nonverbal disagreement, conflict, anger and other signals that not everyone is in sync.

Allow people to finish what they are saying. If someone interrupts direct the conversation back to the previous speaker to let them finish. Ask follow up questions that show the speakers point was heard and that challenge the speaker to finish an incomplete thought. If they are only supposed to listen then inform them at the beginning. Ask everyone to put their mobile phones on vibrate in order to avoid interruptions.

The leader of the meeting is only a facilitator. Their opinion is best expressed by restating or agreeing with the comments made by the ones participating in the meeting. This will encourage the group to take ownership of what is decided. The most effective facilitators also bring a lot of energy to the meeting and a sense of humor. Even the most intense discussion can benefit from a little humor at key moments. The best facilitators are able to advance the agenda gracefully without the participants realizing they are being guided. Facilitators also set the tone in attitude for the meeting. People will seek opportunity to test limits, upstage, divert, entertain and manipulate instead of staying on track. The first time you allow this to happen; you set a precedent and lose credibility.

As Christian leaders we must conduct the meeting with the utmost respect and dignity that is due our fellow workers. Make every effort to discuss issues and do not allow the discussion to become personal attacks. If the meeting gets out of hand and proper etiquette is not observed, then it is the duty of the facilitator to terminate the meeting. In doing so he/she should remind the participants of their duty to honor our Lord Christ in all we do.

Finally everyone needs to understand and agree that everyone will be given the opportunity to participate, sharing their ideas, feelings and concerns in a Christian manner without fear of retaliation or rebuke. Ideas should be received with thanksgiving and each one should be encouraged to participate. An atmosphere of love and appreciation should prevail and it is the leader's job to ensure that this take place. Meetings are necessary, however, they do not have to be unduly long, without purpose or so scary that no one wants to participate. In addition they can and should be conducted on time and in a timely manner, with an agenda and purpose that is clearly stated and understood by all present. Prayerfully asking and allowing the Lord to be present and guiding in our meetings will ensure such meetings will be productive and bring honor and glory to the One whom we serve.

When the meeting has concluded the leader should express his/her appreciation for everyone's attendance. He/she should determine the time and place for a follow up meeting if necessary; and remind everyone of the next scheduled meeting.

Absentees

Inevitably there will be people who fail to attend scheduled meetings. What can be effectively done to make sure they do not miss out on important information without conveying the idea that absenteeism is okay? First determine why they were absent. Were they or a member of their family sick? Was there an emergency? Was there a scheduling conflict? If any of these situations exist then there is a good reason they were unable to attend. In the case of sickness, family emergencies, or death an opportunity to minister presents itself. If the person is chronically absent then a careful confrontation may be needed. In any event, minutes of the procedures, ideas shared, plans made should be kept of the minutes and a copy given to the member who was absent. These should be presented personally by the person leading the meeting. This gives an opportunity to impress upon the absentee the importance of being at meeting when possible and to also convey to them the importance of their role.

Scheduling meeting well in advance of the meeting date and communicating scheduled meetings to all involved will diminish the occurrence of absentees.

-12-

"A Blueprint for Evaluating Leaders"

"...For unto whomsoever much is given, of him shall be much required: and to whom men have committed much, of him they will ask the more."
—Luke 12:48

Evaluations are very important in the educational and leadership realm of the church. Evaluations help us to set goals and identify whether they have been reached. They also help us to identify our strengths and weaknesses, allowing us to make improvements where needed.

Evaluations should never be used to discourage leaders, but rather help to encourage them to never be complacent or satisfied with where they are and what they are doing. Without an honest evaluation of ourselves and the ministries that we lead, we will become mediocre or 'lukewarm'. (Revelation 3:15) Jesus tells us that He doesn't want us to be half-hearted or in the middle. He wants us to be on one side or the other. Jesus desires for us to have a burning passion in the ministry He has called us to and wants us to press forward with an incredible zeal!

Churches should evaluate leadership at least once a year, but must continually evaluate the educational programs in place. Most evaluations are given by the Senior Pastor and/or individuals who would do so with the spirit of God and have knowledge in the area being evaluated. As evaluations take place, leaders must have the opportunity to give their input and respond to matters being discussed. This is also an opportunity for the leader to discuss how the church can respond in order to be more effective in the work.

We have chosen a sample of an evaluation that could be used for evaluating the Director of Christian Education or the Sunday school Superintendent. We believe it is beneficial to allow the Director to evaluate themselves and then compare the results to those doing the evaluation. Following the evaluation process, copies should be kept and results should be revisited at the next evaluation to see where change and improvement have taken place.

Director Evaluation

Name:____________________________________ Date:__________

Position: ____

Rating Scale:	**5 Superior**	Performance is clearly outstanding in all phases of the position. The person's achievements and contributions greatly exceed expectations, standards and requirements.
	4 Above Average	The person consistently performs at a higher level than the job requires.
	3 Average	Performance is satisfactory. The person meets job requirements and expectations.
	2 Below Average	Performance is adequate. The person meets most of the job requirements and expectations but needs improvement.
	1 Unsatisfactory	The person's performance does not meet job requirements or expectations. Improvement is essential.

Rating Performance Areas

______	1.	**Job Knowledge:** Possesses overall knowledge of job; knows duties and responsibilities: seeks additional information and/or training to enhance ability to perform job expectations and sharpen skills and abilities. Comments:
______	2.	**Organization:** Ability to establish schedule of tasks, to prioritize jobs, to accomplish work in a timely fashion and to utilize time in an efficient manner; records and workspace are well ordered. Comments:
______	3.	**Dependability:** Reliability in performance of assigned tasks within allotted time; demonstrates conscientious work behavior; infrequent absences and plans for completion/coverage of job responsibilities when absent. Comments:
______	4.	**Initiative:** Self motivating; resourceful and creative in job performance; strives to develop improved ways of achieving job expectations; willingness to lead and accept more responsibility when needed. Comments:
______	5.	**Decision Making:** Uses logic, good judgment and common sense in job performance and in relating to others Comments:
______	6.	**Adaptability:** Ability to learn and adjust to new ideas and procedures and be flexible in work behavior. Comments:
______	7.	**Responsiveness:** Shows interest in job; friendly and cooperative with coworkers and members of congregation; accepts tasks willingly; works in a professional manner. Comments:
______	8.	**Communication:** Ability to develop effective work relationships; capacity to express ideas clearly; attention to informing staff and church leaders/membership concerning job activities; maintains confidentiality. Comments:
______	9.	**Quality of Work:** Works accurately, neatly and with attention to detail; work is of an acceptable standard. Comments:
______	10.	**Productivity:** Ability to produce a sufficient quantity of work, to work efficiently, and to plan and organize tasks and time. Comments:
		Overall Performance Level (average of the ten "Performance Areas" rated):

Last Year's Goals

	Goal #1	
	Activities to meet goal:	a.
		b.
		c.
	Progress/status of completion:	
	Goal #2	
	Activities to meet goal:	a.
		b.
		c.
	Progress/status of completion:	
	Goal #3	
	Activities to meet goal:	a.
		b.
		c.
	Progress/status of completion:	

Next Year's Goals

	Goal #1	
	Activities to meet goal:	a.
		b.
		c.
	Goal to be achieved by:	(date)
	Goal #2	
	Activities to meet goal:	a.
		b.
		c.
	Goal to be achieved by:	(date)
	Goal #3	
	Activities to meet goal:	a.
		b.
		c.
	Goal to be achieved by:	(date)

Director's Comments____

____

____

____.

Supervisor's Comments ____

____

____

____.

Supervisors Signature: ____

Date: ____________________

Director's Signature: ____

Date: _____________________

Senior Pastor's Signature: ____

Date: _____________________

Teacher Evaluations

From time to time, it will be very important for the Christian Education Director or the Sunday School Director to visit a class in progress. The purpose of these visits is to inform the directors on the progress that is made within each classroom and to evaluate the teacher and the class to ensure teaching effectiveness.

When scheduling a classroom visit, it can be done in two different ways. One way is to slip into a classroom unannounced and briefly evaluate your findings. The Director may only stay for a brief period so that several classes can be observed during that time. During this brief observation, the director can tell much about the learning environment, atmosphere of excitement and teacher involvement.

Another way to observe the teacher and the class is to schedule a date in advance for observation to occur. During this type of observation, the director is with the teacher before students arrive until students have left the class. The director observes the flow of the class, the total learning environment and the teaching ability of the teacher. The Director may take notes on how the teacher can better effectively teach the class. Following the class, the director will schedule a time in which they will sit down and go over the teacher's evaluation. During this time, suggestions can be made and issues can be addressed regarding the class.

We must remember that classes are taught by volunteers and often by teachers with no formal Christian education and training. When evaluation is made, we must remember that the church is not striving for perfection, but for excellence. Excellence is simply doing the best that the person can possibly do.

While going over the observation, the Director must express appreciation to the teacher and affirm them in their position. The Director must explain that the purpose of the evaluation is to help them improve where they are in teaching. Also, the evaluation is to help them identify weak areas, while the Director can make suggestion in how it can be improved. This observation will also serve as an opportunity to bring about problem solving. This is also a great time for the teacher to share personal issues in which the teacher and Director can pray about together.

Here is an example of a Teacher/Classroom Evaluation sheet that a director may use as a guideline for observations. After the evaluation has been discussed, the director and teacher may sign and date it at the bottom. A copy can be made and given to the teacher, while the original can be kept on file. The director can schedule any additional observation times needed. Keeping observations on file at the church can help with follow up visits between the Director and the teacher and serve as a reminder that follow up is vital in the progress of teaching.

Teacher/Classroom Evaluation

Date: ______________________

Teacher: _______________________ Classroom: ___________________

Classroom:

Was the classroom set up and ready for learning? ____________________

____.

Was the atmosphere of the classroom inviting and exciting? ____________

____.

Teacher:

Was the teacher prepared to teach the class? _________________________

____.

Was the lesson material prepared and taught with enthusiasm? __________

____.

Did the teacher use other resources other than the lesson material to teach?

____

____

____.

Did the teacher make the lesson relevant to the student? ________________

____

____.

Did the teacher challenge the student and application suggested? ________

____

____.

Comments/Suggestions: ____

____

____.

(Give teacher one copy and keep original on file.)

Part Five

Maintaining the Structure

-13-

"Blueprint For Avoiding Burnout"

"Come unto me, all ye that labour and are heavy laden, and I will give you rest." —Luke 11:28

Maintaining the Structure

Avoiding Burn Out

If you want something done, ask a busy person and they will get it done! These busy people are "go getters", "accomplishers" and very "driven" in the work they do. What's the natural thing to do? Give someone who is already doing a hundred things one more task. Why? Because we know it will get done. As leaders, we often look at getting the work done and seldom look at the repercussion to the person we are asking.

Susan is a 33 year old mother of two children, ages 5 and 8. She works as a fulltime teller at a local bank and her two children are actively involved in soccer, which requires a weekly practice and a commitment to Saturday games. She and her husband Tom attend at the local church where Tom is a deacon and serves on the budget and finance committee. Susan is the church pianist. As pianist, she must be available for all choir rehearsals and play for every service at her church. She practices with individuals singing solos and duets, and accompanies every seasonal cantata that is scheduled by the choir director. Susan is an outgoing person who is a natural. People 'naturally' are drawn to her smile and winning personality. She is dependable and people know that she will help in any way she can because she loves the Lord!

The Sunday school department is growing and is in need of a third grade teacher on Sunday morning. After being turned down by several members, the director of the Sunday school sees Susan and realizes that she is the obvious choice to take the class. She is fun, loves people and is dedicated to the church therefore she is the perfect choice. Susan is approached and willingly accepts the position of third grade teacher.

Let's take a look at this scenario. We have an individual already very active in the church. As church pianist, she is already giving an over abundance of her time and energy just to maintain her position in the music. She is giving countless hours to choir rehearsals, individual practices and church services. Let's take a look beyond the church...

She works a fulltime job and has two young children. No doubt when she gets off from work at 5:00 pm., she must pick up the children and whisk them away for soccer practice. It's 7:00 and she realizes that her family has not had dinner, so many times it's a trip through a fast food drive thru. After dinner, the children must do their homework and get their baths. Now it's 9:00 and mom still hasn't even changed her clothes. Speaking of clothes, the laundry has stacked up in the laundry room and the bills need to be paid and mailed. Susan goes to bed exhausted at 11:30 only to wake to the alarm at 5:00 am, in which she will repeat another grueling day of activity.

Let's put all of this together with the responsibilities that she has to her home, job and family and you'll see what her life looks like. This type of schedule may go on for a period of time, but will not last because she will not be able to physically and mentally endure it. This scenario is a very familiar one to those who serve within the church. They have full time jobs, have commitments to activities outside the church such as sports, clubs, etc., are very active in the church, yet we want them to do one more thing. When more and more responsibility is place on individuals who are already serving, they often suffer "burn out" and we also end up losing great workers, and often times great church members. Many leaders tend to be judgmental towards those who say 'no' to more responsibility. They assume they understand what the reasoning is without trying to truly understand the other person's perspective. We must remember that those who serve within the Sunday school are volunteers.

What is burn out? How can we identify those within our church who may be suffering 'burn out' and what can we do to avoid it? The job of church leadership is to recognize this within the workers of the church and prevent it from taking place. Church leadership must also realize that many people have trouble saying "no" and are willing to do what ever because they love the church and they love the Lord. While some individuals are able to take on more work, leadership should look at the life of the individual they are pursuing to determine their load of responsibility. The goal is to balance out the work with the people serving, while teaching and training others to help take on the work of the kingdom.

What is Burn Out?

Life is filled with daily stresses and strains, and sometimes we just get tired. Many of us simply need a little bit of down time to recover. When we still feel drained after a good nights sleep, we may be suffering from 'burnout'. Just like a car, we push ourselves past "E" and eventually run out of gas physically, emotionally, and spiritually.

Burnout happens when we are under constant stress without periods of relief. Sometimes we take our bodies through long hours of activity and mental strain, not realizing that we maybe pushing ourselves to the point of no return. Over time, the body and mind become depressed and can loose their ability to bounce back. It is difficult to recover from this sort of physical and mental condition. When you are tired all the time, activities that you once enjoyed become drudgery and before long, you may begin to feel worthless.

Church volunteer burnout is a major problem within the church today. We realize we need others to get the work done, however, we learn that only 20% of a congregation does 80% of the work! Church leadership must be careful to overload workers within the church. What are some of the signs and symptoms of "burn out"? In Paul Van Aukens article *"Understanding Church Burnout"*, he gives us some signs and symptoms of someone on the road to burnout in the church:

The Road to Burnout

* Over Commitment (always in motion);
* Inadequate breaks and rest (continuous ministry involvement);
* Idealistic standards;
* Constant low-grade stress (occasionally interrupted by crisis!)
* Lack of help and assistance;
* Chronic fatigue from pushing oneself ("hitting the wall");
* Strong sense of responsibility, even when others "dropped the ball";
* Guilty feelings about missing church events/activities;
* Heavy job and family responsibilities/expectations;
* Inability (or strong reluctance) to say no.

Burnout can happen to anyone. In the church, burnout happens to the most dedicated, loyal servant who truly wants to help in ministry. They are constantly challenged with the activities taking place within the position they are serving, while struggling with the lack of knowledge and training to do that position. Also, we must not forget the stress that is place on the leader to fulfill the "visual" responsibilities of the position such as being present for all church events, activities, church services, visitation and meetings.

Sometimes the pastor and staff get a bit out of touch with volunteer busyness. They're so busy (and under-appreciated) themselves, chronic over commitment is simply a way of life. Many leaders within the church want to create an atmosphere so that the congregation assumes everything is running smoothly. Many times, the church fails to recognize the tremendous sacrifice that is taking place with volunteers. Those that do realize the true sacrifice wants no part of.

Steps the Church Can Take Avoid Volunteer Burnout

* *When placing individual in ministry positions, only allow them to lead in one area.*

Often times, Christian people are more than willing to serve where needed. A typical "type A" personality who is driven, competitive and achievement-oriented may be more than willing to serve in several areas, all at one time. When individuals are only allowed to lead in one area of ministry, they will lead more effectively and efficiently. You cannot lead in 3 or 4 areas and give the time and attention to them they deserve. In the church, it is better to have 5 ministries that are strong and solid, than it is to have 20 that barely exist. Setting guidelines for leading ministries will allow members to participate and enjoy other ministries without taking full responsibility of them.

* *Allow Leaders to make a "Time Commitment"*

When asking individuals to step into a leading position such as a Sunday school teacher, ask for a 6-month or a 12-month commitment. After the time commitment has been fulfilled, allow them the opportunity to "roll off" or serve for another time period. Sometimes, individuals go through periods in their lives where things happen that will take their time and attention. When a leader knows in advance what the commitment entails, they are more likely to stick to their commitment. Giving a time commitment will allow them to "freely" step out of their position if necessary without feeling like they are breaking their commitment.

* *Properly Educate & Train Your Volunteers*

Sunday school teachers are volunteers with little or no training. One of the biggest factors teachers deal with is frustration because they don't know what to do. Before placing the teacher into the classroom, they must be trained. The church must provide training sessions that will give them all of the necessary tools for teaching that class, while giving them vital information to ensure its effectiveness. Teachers must be aware of what is expected of them as well as what they should expect from the church. Sunday school training should also keep them updated on new teaching techniques, ideas and other resources. Training is an ongoing process that should take place on a quarterly or even a monthly basis. Training sessions should allow teachers to receive updated information for their class and get motivated about teaching others about Christ!

* *Communicate, Communicate, Communicate*

One important task that the Sunday school director has is to communicate with the teacher. It is a good idea to speak to them not only on an "ongoing" basis, but also scheduling to meet with them one on one at least once a month. They should be available to check in with each teacher from time to time and say, "Do you need anything?" "Is there anything I can do for you?" The director should be the eyes and ears, while stopping to look and listen to what is going on around them. They should observe the attitude of not only the students in the Sunday school, but the teacher as well. When meeting with the teacher one on one, the director should take the opportunity to minister to them by praying with them and encouraging them. This is also the time to help the teacher resolve any conflicts or problems they may have in the classroom. The director can give helpful ideas and resources for that specific age group and teacher.

* *Provide Opportunities to Renew and Refresh Themselves Spiritually*

Every leader in the church should be given the opportunity to participate in events and activities without responsibilities. Teachers should be given the opportunity to attend classes, services, etc…not to lead or teach, but to enjoy! Jesus Himself found time to get alone with God. A time to think, rest and just enjoy being in the presence of God! Sometimes leaders need to do what Jesus told the apostles in Mark 6:31… *"Come ye yourselves apart into a desert place, and rest a while".* Sunday school teachers are volunteers who often work full-time jobs on top of all of their responsibilities at church. They give what little time they have. We must protect our teachers and leaders by providing opportunities to be refreshed and renewed spiritually and physically.

A great way to refresh your teachers is to offer a prayer retreat weekend in which the team finds a secluded place to get away, pray, read their Bibles, and find rest and renewal. Another great way is to allow the teacher to come out of the classroom at least once a month and allow their assistants to teach the class. The teacher can attend a class of their choice, breaking up their normal church routine.

In Closing

Christian education is a lifelong process that requires continuous effort. We should always keep in mind that we are looking for lasting results and therefore we should not lose patience. We are responsible for planting and watering, and must always trust God for the increase.

To accomplish these results requires two key elements; organization and evaluation. Just as God had a plan when He created the universe, we must have a plan that will focus our efforts on the desired results. We must also continually evaluate the process, making changes as needed. Evaluation must be constant, immediate, honest and constructive.

How do I start? Start with the people you have and the resources that are available to you. Build a solid foundation with these two elements and you will have made a tremendous first step. With a solid foundation, the building process can truly begin.

We must always remember that our measure of success is not necessarily God's measure of success. Not every church is meant to be a mega church and not every Sunday school is meant to be a mega Sunday school. We are responsible to disciple those that God has entrusted to us and should stay focused on this task without comparing ourselves to other churches.

We pray that this book will inform and inspire those of you who have accepted the call to teach. We also pray that God will encourage you through this work, and will continue to provide all that you need as you serve Him. It is our desire to see Sunday school once again play a major role in the salvation of souls and the building of disciples.

Book Sources

Chapter 1—A Blueprint For Planning & Goal Setting

1. Dr. Elmer Towns, *The Sunday School Encyclopedia*, Tyndale House Publishing; January 1993 Adapted from V. Gilbert Beers, *Family Bible Library* (Nashville; Southwestern, 1971)

2. James Smart, *The Teaching Ministry of the Church*, Philidelphia, Westminster Press 1954, pg 107 .

Chapter 2—A Blueprint For Selecting Leaders

1. The Big Book of Job Descriptions For Ministry: Gospel Light 2002

2. *Ibid*

Chapter 3—A Blueprint For Selecting Teachers

1. Thomas J. Cook *The Sunday School Page, www.sschool.com*

Chapter 5—A Blueprint For Creative Methods

1. *Teaching Techniques,* Evangelical Training Association 1983

2. Ibid., pg 20

3. Ibid., pg 21

4. Findley B. Edge, *Teaching For Results* (Nashville-Broadman-Holman Publishers, 1995

Chapter 6—Understanding the Blueprint

1. Grace Ketterman and Herbert Ketterman, *The Complete Book of Baby and Child Care For Christian Parents* (Old Tappan, N,J.: Revell, 1982), p. 149.

2. Florence Conner Hearn, Guiding Preschoolers (Nashville: Convention, 1969), p.19

3. Clark, Brubaker & Zuck, *Childhood Education In The Church* (Moody Press 1986), p. 89

4. Eleanor L. Doan, *It's Never Too Early* (Ventura, Calif,: Gospel Light, 1967) p.3

5. Meryl Welch, *Cradle Roll Handbook* (Schaumburg, Ill.: Regular Baptist, 1979) p. 3.

6. Lewis, Frank "New Beginnings" *Let's Worship Magazine*, (Spring 2003): 67-68

7. Clark, Brubaker & Zuck, *Childhood Education In the Church* (Moody Press 1986), p. 100

8. Ibid, pg 100

9. Adapted from V. Gilbert Beers, *Family Bible Library* (Nashville: Southwestern, 1971), 10:14-15

10. Ibid

Chapter 7—Understanding the Blueprints of Preschoolers

1. Adapted from V. Gilbert Beers, *Family Bible Library* (Nashville: Southwestern, 1971) 18-19

Chapter 8—Understanding the Blueprints of Elementary Students

1. Adapted from V. Gilbert Beers, *Family Bible Library* (Nashville; Southwestern, 1971)

2. Clark, Brubaker & Zuck *Childhood Education In the Church* (Moody Press 1986) pg. 138

3. Ibid

Chapter 9—Understanding the Blueprints for Middlers & Teens

1. Departments of Health and Human Services, www.cdc.gov

2. Adapted from V. Gilbert Beers, *Family Bible Library* (Nashville; Southwestern, 1971)

3. *You And Your Sixth Grader,* University of Iowa;

4. *Child and Your Health, www.cyh.com*

5. Ibid

6. Research Facts and Findings, A collaboration of Cornell University, University of Rochester, and the New York State Center for School Safety; May 2004

7. American Academy of Child and Adolescent Psychiatry, Washington D.D.

8. Growth and Development, Ages 11-14 Years; Healthbanks.com

Chapter 10—Understanding the Blueprints for Young Adults

1. American Academy of Child and Adolescent Psychiatry, Washing D.C.

2. Growth and Development, Ages 15-18 Years; Healthbanks.com

3. Cognitive Development Between 15-18 Years; Amy Fackler, MA Healthwise 1995

4. Adolescent Growth & Development; Angela Huebner; Virginia Tech

5. Research Facts and Finds; A collaboration of Cornell University, University of Rochester, and the New York State Center for School Safety; May 2004

Chapter 11—Blueprints for Evaluating the Structure

1. Faith Sunday School Evaluation; flbaptist.org

Chapter 13—Blueprint For Avoiding Burnout

1. Understand Church Burnout and What to Do About It; Phil Van Auken *Church Administration July 1996*

Book Resources

Raney, Deborah and Vicky Miller. *More Childrens Sermons to Go: 52 Take Home Lessons About God.* Abingdon Press, 2001.

Maxwell, John. *Developing the Leader Within You.* Thomas Nelson, 2001

Hybels, Bill. *Courageous Leadership. Zondervan, 2002.*

Lefever, Marlene. *Creative Teaching Methods.* Cook Communications

Hendricks, Dr. Howard. *Teaching to Change Lives.* Multnormah Pub.Inc, 2003

Gilbert, Dr. Larry and Cindy Spear. *The Big Book of Job Descriptions for Ministry.* Gospel Light, 2001.

Haystead, Wes, Sheryl Haystead and Wesley Haystead. *How To Have A Great Sunday School.* Gospel Light, 1999.

Towns, Elmer L. *What Every Sunday School Teacher Should Know.* Gospel Light, 2001.

Jones, Idris W. and Ruth L. Spencer *The Workbook of the Sunday School Superintendent.* Judson Press, Revised Edition, 1994.

Johnston, Ray *Help! I'm A Sunday School Teacher.* Zondervan, April, 1996.

Bowden, Boyce A. *The Child Friendly Church.* Abingdon Press, 1999.

Wideman, Jim. *Children's Ministry Leadership.* Group Publishing 2003.

Gospel Lights Really Big Book of Kid Sermons & Object Talks w/CD Rom. 2004.

Big Book of Kid Sermons and Bible Talks. Gospel Light 1999.

Jutila, Craig . *Leadership Essentials for Children's Ministry.* Flagship Church Resources: Nov. 2001.

Barna, George. *Transforming Children Into Spiritual Champions.* Group Pub: June 1, 2003

Little Blessings Nursery Smart Pages. Gospel Light 1997.

Haystead, Sheryl. *Early Childhood Smart Pages (Ages 2-5)* Gospel Light 2002.

Haystead, Sheryl. *Sunday School Smart Pages.* Gospel Light 1992.

Haystead, Wesley. *5th & 6th Grade Smart Pages.* Gospel Light 1996.

Children's Ministry Smart Pages w/CD Rom. Gospel Light 1996.

Sunday School Promo Pages. Gospel Light 1993

Reed, Millard. *It's Your Serve: A Practical Leadership for Pastors & Sunday School Superintendents.* Beacon Hill Press 1989.

Johnson, Talmadge and Stan Johnson. *Rediscovering the Sunday School.* Beacon Hill Press 2000.

Haston, Wayne. *Adult Sunday School Ministry: The Dynamics of Successful Classes.* Pathway Press 1993.

Hemphill, Ken. *Revitalizing the Sunday Morning Dinosaur.* Broadman/Holman 1996.

Halverson, Delia. *32 Ways to Become A Great Sunday School Teacher.* Abingdon Press 1997.

Sunday School CPR. Abingdon Press 1998.

Sunday School Attendance Boosters: 165 Fresh & New Ideas. Group Publishing 2000.

Furnish, Dorothy Jean. *Exploring the Bible with Children.* Nashville: Abingdon, 1975.

Hunt, Gladys. *One for a Child's Heart.* Grand Rapids: Zondervan, 1969.

Bolton, Barbara J., and Charles T. Smith. *Creative Bible Learning for Children.* Ventura, Calif.; Gospel Light, Regal Books, 1977.

Rives, Elsie, and Ann Tonks. *Bible Teaching for Children Through the Sunday School.* Nashville: Convention, 1984.

Towns, Elmer. *The Successful Sunday School and Teachers Guidebook.* Carol Stream, Ill.: Creation House, 1976.

Zuck, Roy B. *The Holy Spirit in Your Teaching.* Rev. and enlarged ed. Wheaton, Ill.: Scripture Press, Victor Books, 1985.

Gangel, Kenneth O. *24 Ways to Improve Your Teaching*. Wheaton, Ill.: Scripture Press, Victor Books, 1974.

Show Me The Story. Flannelgraph kit. Minneapolis: Augsburg, 1981.

Tobey, Katherine. *Learning and Teaching through the Senses.* Philadelphia: Westminister, 1970.

Lingo, Susan. *200+ Activities for Children's Ministry.* Standard Publishing Company, March 1999.

Roehlkepartain, Jolene L. *Fidget Busters: 101 Quick Attention-Getters for Children's Ministry.* Group Publishing. December 1991.

Morgan, Tony and Tim Stevens. *Simply Strategic Volunteers: Empowering People For Ministry.* Group Publishing, December 2004.

Richards, Lawrence O. *Children's Ministry.* Zondervon, Reprint Ed. September 1988.

Shaffer, David R. *Social & Personality Developnebt.* Wadsworth Publishing. 4th Edition. July 30, 1999.
Everyone's A Winner: Games for Children. Group Publishing. June 1995.
Parrish, Bo. *Building A Children's Ministry.* Tate Publishing & Enterprises. April 1, 2006.
Ritchhart, Lisa Ashley. *Start An Effective Nursery/Toddler Ministry.* Warner Press. April, 2000.
Stanley, Andy, Lane Jones and Reggie Joiner. *Seven Practices of Effective Ministry.* Multnomah, August 18, 2004.
Stanley, Andy. *The Next Generation Leader.* Multonomah, January 1, 2003.
Griggs, Donald L. *Christian Education in the Small Church.* Judson Press, April 1988.
Bastian, Karl, K. Christie Bowler, LA Dona Hein, Jerry Hull, Rick Osborne, Janet Teitsort.
The Ultimate Bible Guild for Children's Ministry. Group Publishing, January 1999.
Miller, Sue and David Staal. *Making Your Children's Ministry the Best Hour of Every Kid's Week.* Zondervan, April 1, 2004.
Children's Ministry Guide For Smaller Churches. Group Publishing, September 1995.
Roehlkepartain, Jolene L. *Children's Ministry That Works!* Group Publishing, May 1991.
The Craft of Christian Teaching. Judson Press, December 1998.
Richards, Lawrence O. and Gary J. Bredfeldt. *Creative Bible Teaching.* Moody Press. March 1998.
Jutila, Craig. *The Growing Leader.* Group Publishing. December 2003
Creative Storytelling Guide for Children's Ministry. Standard Publishing. Nov. 2003.
James, Steven. *Sharable Parables: Creative Storytelling Ideas for Ages 3-12.* Standard Publishing. January 30, 2005.
Mercadante Frank. *Growing Teen Disciples.* Saint Mary's Press. September 2002.
Fields, Doug. *Purpose Driven Youth Ministry.* Zondervan (January 1, 1998.
Fields, Doug. *Your First Two Years In Youth Ministry.* Zondervan (August 1, 2002)
McDowell, Josh and Bob Hostetler. *Handbook on Counseling Youth.* W. Publishing June 11, 1996.
Parrott III, Dr. Les. *Helping the Struggling Adolescent.* Zondervan, Revised & Expanded edition; June 1, 2000.

Towns, Elmer L. *Teaching Teens.* Baker Book House. January 1, 1965.
Curie, Barbara. *77 Dynamic Ideas for Teaching the Bible to Teens.* Standard Publishing 1977.
Johnston, Ray. *Help! I'm A Sunday School Teacher.* Zondervan. April 1, 1996.
Bruce, Barbara. *Teaching Children Bible Basics.* Abingdon Press. November 1999.
Bruce, Barbara. *7 Ways of Teaching the Bible to Children.* Abingdon Press. October 1996
Towns, Elmer L. and Stan Toler. *What Every Pastor Should Know About Sunday School.* Regal Books. December 2002.
Foreman, Brian. *Help! I Teach Youth Sunday School.* Smyth & Helwys Publishing. March 2004.
Murray, Dick. *Teaching the Bible to Adults & Youth.* Abingdon Press; Rev. & Updated edition; March 1993.
Stoner, Marcia. *Teaching Tips for Terrified Teachers.* Abingdon Press. January 1999.

Web Resources

www.SundaySchool.com - a website offering curriculum resources

www.kidssundayschool.com - a website offering children's ministry, children's church and Sunday school teacher resources

www.ebibleteacher.com - resources for lesson preparation and presentation

www.lifeway.com - bookstore of the Southern Baptist Convention

www.sschool.com - Sunday school and Church growth administration helps

www.thewiredword.com - Sunday school lesson that confront the news with scripture and hope

www.sundayschoolhelp.com - provides information resources and training for Sunday school teachers and leaders

www.biblekidsfunzone.com - Bible crafts for children, Sunday school lessons, etc

www.christianedwarehouse.com - Sunday school, VBS, Bible clubs, education resources

Appendix

Interview Strategy

It is the contention of the authors that for the most part, our Sunday schools have done an inadequate job in teaching our children the basics of Bible knowledge. In an effort to prove or disprove this hypothesis, a survey was conducted by the authors among various members of various churches. These members constituted every walk of life, many different experiences, varied positions in the church and of all age groups. A sample of the survey is included in the appendix of this book. The results of the survey were very interesting and it is the opinion of the authors that cur point is proven. In addition interviews were conducted by the authors in an effort to discover what people value the most in Sunday school. Two basic questions were asked: "What is it that has made the greatest impact upon your life in your Sunday school experience and what is it that you desire Sunday school to do for your child?"

Subject One: Ashley. He is thirty-two years of age and has been a Christian approximately ten years. His Sunday school experience has been during his adulthood.

1. He is impressed by the opportunity to interact and discuss various issues in class. He believes you can learn from others as much as from the teacher.
2. He feels his Sunday School experience in preparing him for life, although he wishes there were more instruction on how to study and interpret the Bible.
3. He wants Sunday school to teach his child:
   A. what is the purpose of Sunday school
   B. about Christ
   C. how to interact with other and reach people for Christ.

4. He feels it is essential for the church to assist parents in developing parenting skills and helping their child to develop spiritually.

5. He characterizes his Sunday School experience as being very positive.

Subject Two: Amy. She is thirty years of age, was saved at the age of seven and spent her development years in Sunday school in a Missionary Baptist Church.

1. Her most profound memory is of a teacher she had as a child. He stressed Bible knowledge and memorization. He was involved in her life outside the church setting. He lived a godly life in front of the people.
2. Would characterize her Sunday School experience as positive and influential in helping her become the person she is today.
3. She wants the Sunday School to teach her child that Christ is the most important thing in life and having a consistent relationship with Him makes life better.

Neither of these people could give me a definitive answer as to how they would design a Sunday school. This could be because each one has had a positive experience and feels their Sunday school experience has met the needs of their life. As I interviewed these people I was struck by how much the relationship aspect of Sunday school made a big impact upon their lives. Both related to me the impact that others in Sunday school had upon them. Amy remembered one teacher who was involved in her life outside the classroom setting and outside the church setting. This demonstrated to her that this teacher had a bigger agenda than just teaching a lesson on Sunday morning. He was interested in her as a person.

This is the idea we must convey to our teaching staff. Sunday school teaching is more than just getting through a lesson. It involves teaching and relating to those who are sitting in our classroom. Jesus was a relational person. Often he would build a relationship with those whom society had cast aside or who were poor in spirit. Sunday school teachers have a great opportunity to show their students how much God loves them by living in relationship with them in and out of the classroom setting. Sunday School teachers should know their students, become familiar with their home life and be willing to invest time in their lives.

Mrs. Scott conducted other interviews. She also discovered a direct correlation between a positive Sunday school experience and the person or persons that led the classes and taught the lessons. Following are her findings:

The Sunday School Experience

I interviewed four individuals who shared very positive experiences in Sunday school. Their responses to the questions reveal how Sunday school has met their needs in a very specific way;

Question: What was one of your most profound memory of Sunday school?

Virginia - Sunday school has been where I've received answers to many of my own personal questions. It wasn't until I learned about Scripture and how it applies to my life that I received the answers to the questions that I had pondered on or had asked God.

Steve - My most profound memory of Sunday school was an object lesson that was taught to us by our 10th grade boys Sunday school teacher called "The Gospel In A Nutshell". It explained the plan of salvation. Now when I see a nut, I am reminded of the plan of salvation.

Susan - Two things were memorable for me…Sunday school was where I learned many biblical principles in my life. For example, this was where "tithing" was taught to me and why it was important. In Sunday school, we were able to learn about it and discover what God's Word said. Also, the Sunday school enabled relationship, which brought about fellowship and encouragement.

Question: *How valuable do you think Sunday school is?

Debbie - Sunday school is very valuable, especially in the early years because that is where the foundation is laid for children. The Bible must be taught on different age levels for better understanding. In a corporate worship, that is more of a celebration of what God is doing or has already done. In corporate worship, the Word is not broken down and taught for personal meaning. In Sunday school, this is where the 'meat' of the Bible is taught for understanding and application.

Virginia - Sunday school is more valuable than a worship service. This is where you get to know God, learn about God and build upon His Word. This is the foundation of learning!

Steve - A Christian education is priceless. Kids learn to go to church just like they learn to go to school. They develop a habit of making time to learn God's Word. They also surround themselves with friends who share in their love of Christ or share in the knowledge that they have of Christ. For adults, there is so much anti-Christian activity going on such as not being able to put up nativity scenes or say "Merry Christmas" in various places, they must surround themselves with the same Christian influences. A Sunday school not only becomes a 'safe' place to build relationships with others who loves Christ, but a place where you can learn solid Biblical teachings that will enable you to stand firm on what you believe.

Susan - Sunday school is extremely important. Sunday school is where you connect with individuals, getting the encouragement and support that you can't get in a worship service. The Sunday school is also a place where you can dig deeper into the Word of God and learn more for your own spiritual growth. This is where you get the 'meat and meaning' of the Word.

Question: *How effective has Sunday school been in your life?

Debbie - Without Sunday school, I would not have a foundational knowledge of the Bible. As an adult, I am able to build upon this foundation for deeper meaning and better understanding.

Virginia - Sunday school has allowed me to grow as a Christian. Because of that, it has influenced me as a woman, mother, wife, friend, etc...

Susan - I did not attend church until I was older, but my very first exposure to the church and to Christ was through a Sunday school effort. I lived in town and a church was planning a Vacation Bible School at their church and had come into my neighborhood and invited me to come. If I had Sunday school, I would have made better decisions and better choices. I love my parents and feel very grateful for all they have done, but one thing that would have made it perfect was for them to have taken me to Sunday school.

Question: *Knowing what you know about Sunday school, what do you want the Sunday school to do for your child?

Debbie - I want Sunday school to teach my child about the Bible and how she can apply it. When she attends corporate worship, she can have a better understanding of what is taking place.

Virginia - I would want Sunday school to give them a firm foundation to build on. If they are open to studying and applying it, it will change their lives!

Steve - I don't want the Sunday school to be the only place they learn about the Bible, but it should be a support to what I am teaching them at home. The Sunday school can support and encourage parents to teach godly values at home.

Question: *If you could design a Sunday school, how would you do it?

Debbie - I would make it more age appropriate and in-depth on their level. Many churches focus on 'having fun', which I think it should be, but with more emphasis on learning.

Virginia - I would do all classes in small groups and during the Sunday school hour. This allows more concentrated teaching for each age group and allows more opportunity for discussion. Also, I would group classes with common needs; for example: widowed adults, parents who have lost children, singles, etc…

Steve - Every arm of the church that is successful has to have a champion. That champion has to be sold out and completely committed to it. They have to know the Bible and not just give opinions. They must be involved in the lives of those within the class because this shows they care about the lives of their students. The teachers must receive on going training to teach and have classes that are small and personal.

Susan - I would have smaller classes and teach more application and not just do's and don'ts. When you teach application, you are also teaching them how to build a better personal relationship with Christ and how to love Him. I would encourage more social involvement with the class doing more things together and becoming more involved in each others lives. This helps build relationships and accountability among those in class. Teachers must spend time with their students.

Basic Bible Knowledge Results

A quiz that consisted of twenty questions of basic bible knowledge was given. Examples of these questions are included in the appendix of this book. Eighty-nine of the quizzes were returned with the following results.

Out of the eighty-nine respondents only two answered 100 percent of the questions correctly. Seventy-three of those who took the quiz missed ten or less of the questions. Fourteen answered between eleven and eighteen of the questions incorrectly. If a passing grade consists of answering at least fourteen questions correctly, then only fifty-two of the eighty-nine total participants made a passing grade. While this is slightly more than half of the students it means nearly half of those tested failed. Granted these questions did not address any moral issues and does not reflect on whether or not the persons are applying biblical standards to their lives, but it does reveal the failure of the church to teach in an effective way the basic things of the bible. This would not be acceptable in secular education and should be alarming to those of us who are in Christian education. It means that we must do a better job of educating and training those who are under our care.

But how are we to do that job? What needs to take place in order for this to happen in our church world? There needs to be a serious, objective look at how we do Sunday school and all the other Christian education programs in the church. Class procedures, curriculum choices, teaching methods and personnel need to be examined to see if we are effectively teaching the facts, truths and principles of the Bible. We need to ask the tough questions. We need to get beyond the status quo and get serious about the task that is before us. Our Lord and Savior Jesus Christ gave us the command to "...make disciples teaching them to observe all things that I have commanded you." Are we doing that? Are we making disciples? Or are we merely spending time?

The Basic Bible Knowledge Quiz reveals that we can and must do better in indoctrinating our class members in the Word of God. The fact that many people do not feel they know how to effectively use the Bible to answer their everyday problems. And the fact that while many people claim to be Christian their lifestyles do not reflect their expressed faith demands that we as Christian educators must examine our work and then make changes where necessary.

Someone may say that the interviews and Bible knowledge quiz were not very scientific. The authors do not dispute that but they do affirm that the interviews and quiz underscore the importance of Sunday school for impacting lives for Christ and they underscore the idea that we must do a better job of teaching Biblical truths and principles to those who are given to our care.

Basic Bible Knowledge

1. Who was the first woman?
   a. Mary
   b. Eve
   c. Ruth
   d. Sarah

2. His brothers sold him into slavery, but he became very important in Egypt when he was older.
   a. Benjamin
   b. Abraham
   c. Isaac
   d. Joseph

3. Because he was so little, this man climbed a tree so he could see Jesus when he came to town. Then Jesus came to his house for tea!
   a. Paul
   b. Zacchaeus
   c. David
   d. Benjamin

4. This woman entered a beauty contest and married a King!
   a. Mary
   b. Eve
   c. Esther
   d. Ruth

5. Who baptized Jesus?
   a. John
   b. Luke
   c. Matthew
   d. Mark

6. According to John, what were the last three words that Jesus said before He died?
   a. Father, forgive them
   b. It is finished
   c. I am thirsty
   d. Behold your son

True or False

7. Adam and Eve's two sons were Cain and Abel. ________________

8. Noah built the ark out of poplar wood. __________________

9. Matthew was the Gospel writer who was a doctor. ________________

10. Joseph was known as the Man of Patience. _____________________

11. The Bible is divided into 2 sections, New Testament and Old Testament and contains 65 Books. ________________________

12. In a parable told by Jesus, a Levite helped a man who had been robbed and wounded. __________________________

Fill in the Blank

_______________ was the man who was converted to Christianity on the road to Damascus.

Joseph and Mary were in Bethlehem when Jesus was born because ____.

Although we don't know for certain how many wise men came to visit Jesus, but the Bible does tell us they came from the _____________ . (direction)

In II Timothy, Paul said we should "Study to shew thyself ____________ unto God."

Noah was in the ark for _______________________ (how long?)

Lazarus had two sisters named _____________ and _______________.

There are ____________ tribes of the children of Israel.

Jesus called _________ Disciples to "follow" Him.

About the Authors

Donald W. Key

Rev. Donald Key and his wife Frances have been married for 35 years. They have a daughter Janet who is married to John Rowland. They reside in Franklin, KY. John and Janet have two children Preston and Maura. Don is a graduate of Oakland City University. He has pastured churches in Indiana, Kentucky and Tennessee. He and Frances served as missionaries to the country of Honduras, Central America from 2002-2005. Don, along with Rev. Glenn Jenkins, co-founded Christian Training Institute, which is dedicated to making training available, affordable and accessible to pastors, teachers and other church leaders. Don served as President and was on the teaching faculty of CTI for nine years. Presently he is pastor of New Vision Ministries in Westmoreland, TN. Don has always had a passion for Christian education and hopes this book will be a blessing to all that read it. He appreciates very much the opportunity to collaborate with Carol Scott (one of the greatest Christian educators he knows) in the development of this book. May God grant us all a passion for making disciples through Christian education.

Carol Scott

Carol Scott holds a bachelor's degree in Religious Education from Bethany Bible College and Theological Seminary. She serves on the Board of Directors of Christian Training Institute, where she has taught education and church growth classes for the past 9 years. She leads conferences in the areas of Sunday school, Family issues and Women's Ministries. Her hearts desire is to train leaders to become more effective as they minister in the local church. She and her husband Mark have been married for 24 years and have one son Andrew who is a junior at Austin Peay State University.

Printed in the United States
76057LV00006B/1-75

9 781424 158607